TWENTIETH
CENTURY
WORLD
HISTORY

# THE CARIBBEAN

## IN THE TWENTIETH CENTURY

**JOHN GRIFFITHS**

Batsford Academic and Educational *London*

# CONTENTS

## ACKNOWLEDGMENT

The Author and Publishers thank the following for their kind permission to reproduce copyright illustrations: Associated Press Ltd for figs 2, 10, 15, 16, 26, 33, 45; BBC Hulton Picture Library for figs 9, 19, 36, 37; Camera Press Ltd for figs 3, 5, 6, 11, 24, 48, 49; Keystone Press Agency Ltd for figs 20, 25, 27, 34; Popperfoto for figs 7, 8, 13, 17, 18, 22, 23, 28, 29, 30, 31, 35, 38, 39, 46. The map on page 3 was drawn by R.F. Brien. Figs 4, 12, 21, 32, 40, 41, 42, 43 and 44 are copyright of the Author.

*For Paul Abercrombie, the fifth brother*

© John Griffiths 1984
First published 1984

Typeset by Tek-Art Ltd, Kent
and printed in Spain by
Grijelmo S.A., Bilbao
for the publishers
Batsford Academic and Educational,
an imprint of B. T. Batsford Ltd,
4 Fitzhardinge Street
London W1H 0AH

ISBN 0 7134 3839 8

# GEOGRAPHICAL PERSPECTIVES

Trinidadian slaves of the nineteenth century believed that when God made the world he shook the earth from his fingers and so made the West Indies. More prosaicly, the Trinidadian historian C.L.R. James has referred to the area as "nothing but bits of dirt in the Caribbean sea".

The Caribbean is one of the most diverse regions of the world whose history, more than most, has been greatly influenced by its geography. The area known as the Caribbean stretches from Mexico in the North, through Central America to Venezuela, Guyana (formerly British Guiana), Suriname, and French Guyana in the South. The thousands of tiny islands which make up the Caribbean archipelago, and which are most commonly thought of in connection with anything Caribbean, stretch in a line from the Florida peninsula to South America itself. If one includes the Bahamas in our picture of the Caribbean, then there is an Atlantic outpost as well.

There are some fifty inhabited Caribbean islands in the chain, ranging in size from Cuba (the size of England with a population of nearly 10 million) and Hispaniola (made up of Haiti and the Dominican Republic just over half the size of Cuba) to small islands like Bequia close to St Vincent in the Eastern Caribbean, with a land

**1   The Caribbean.**

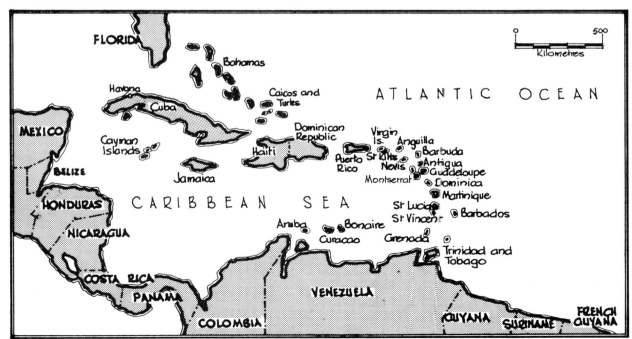

area of just seven square miles and a population of about three thousand. Most of the Caribbean islands are small, a factor that has influenced both economic and social developments and contributed to the notorious isolationism of the islands.

The larger, Northern, islands – Cuba, Jamaica and Hispaniola (Haiti and the Dominican Republic) – make up the Greater Antilles. The smaller, Eastern islands – Anguilla, Antigua, Martinique, Guadeloupe, Dominica, St Lucia, Barbados and the Grenadines – make up the Lesser Antilles. During the days of sail, when the Caribbean was of great importance in the trade winds belt, the northerly islands were known as the Leeward Islands, those to the East as the Windwards. These labels continue to the present day, as does the term "West Indies", though the latter term, linked as it is to former colonial days of British rule in the Caribbean, has taken on a pejorative meaning and is falling out of use. There may be no West Indies, but there are many West Indians.

The variation in size of the different islands, and the imbalance of resources and power that this implies, has been an important factor in the fragmentation of the region. Though the distances from island to island are not great, and although there is now good air and sea transportation and communication, the insularity within the region persists. It has often been said of migrants from the Caribbean that they would meet more of their neighbours on the journey to Southampton, lasting a matter of days, than they would in the same number of years at home.

Most of the Caribbean lies within the Northern Tropics. The fertility of the soil, the constant warm climate and the long growing seasons have made possible the monocultural development of the area for which it is now famous. The lushness of the vegetation, which so impressed Columbus, and the richness, diversity and beauty of the islands have all contributed to the image of the idyllic life of the Caribbean, which modern tourist advertising seems determined to perpetuate.

Yet there is another side to the Caribbean, a sting in the tail. For the islands of the Caribbean archipelago are volcanic in origin and still capable of eruption. St Pierre in Martinique was destroyed in the eruption of Mt Pelee in 1902. Kingston, Jamaica was destroyed by earthquake and tidal

2  Victims of Hurricane Hattie, which struck Belize in 1961, line up for food, watched over by Jamaican troops brought in to maintain law and order.

wave in 1907. More immediate concerns, however, are the hurricanes which regularly occur in the Summer and Autumn Hurricane Season. The history of the Caribbean is punctuated by hurricane disasters: Puerto Rico's coffee industry was destroyed in 1899; Belize itself in 1931; Grenada's nutmeg crop was dashed to the ground in 1955; Haiti and Cuba were devastated by hurricanes in 1963; Cuba again in 1979 when Hurricane "Allen" swept through the entire region. Not only was Cuba damaged; 97% of St Lucia's banana plantations were destroyed, 95% of St Vincent's, 75% of Dominica's and 40% of. Grenada's. The worst effects of hurricane damage can be mitigated by efficient weather forecasting, and there are hurricane warning centres within the Caribbean, but hurricanes cannot be avoided.

Although the popular image of the Caribbean is one of picturesque islands, this is but one part of the region. Proximity to the US, to Mexico, to Central and Latin America has been an important factor in the development of the region and continues to be so. Countries like Mexico in the North and Venezuela in the South identify with the Caribbean because they are part of it. Their resources, in recent years, have given them a special and closer role in the development of the Caribbean. The United States, whilst clearly not a part of the Caribbean, nevertheless has parts of its territory actually *in* it.

The twentieth-century history of the Caribbean has been increasingly bound up with its contact with the United States. Was it only accident, for example, that caused President Reagan in 1979, in his first foreign policy speech, to refer to the area as "the Mediterranean"? The area has come to be seen as the US Mediterranean. Throughout the nineteenth century successive American Presidents looked with interest at the Caribbean. At the end of the nineteenth century the United

States took Cuba and Puerto Rico from Spain, so acquiring its first foothold in the area. Between the wars the United States consolidated its influence, after which, with the collapse of British interest and power in the region, it has become the paramount external influence. America's influence in the region can be seen through its economic links. In 1982 US investments in the region, excluding Puerto Rico which has a special relationship with the US, were some $4.5 thousand million. In the 1970s, 55% of Caribbean exports and 43% of imports were to and from the United States.

The Cuban Revolution has intensified the interest in the region of the United States, which is determined to ensure that such a revolution does not occur again. Its economic and other pressures on the infant revolutions of Nicaragua and Grenada from 1979, resulting in the invasion of Grenada in 1983, and against the Jamaican government of Michael Manley (which fell in 1979

**3   Seven Mile Beach, Grand Cayman Island. Sun, unspoilt beaches and seclusion are the tourist vision of the Caribbean.**

largely because of US influence) are but some of the manifestations of this policy.

The Caribbean was always seen as strategic to US interests. The threat posed by a Socialist Cuba was always described in strategic terms. The Cuban Missile Crisis of 1962 was an obvious threat to the United States. Less obvious, perhaps, is the degree of control that Cuba could exert over trade routes to the United States, all the busiest of which border Cuba. Since 1973, and OPEC's raising of petrol prices, control of these routes has been of especial concern to the United States, together with the new position which the Caribbean occupies because of its oil resources. There are major oil refineries in Mexico, Venezuela, Puerto Rico, Trinidad and Curacao, all refining oil for the US market. The much-publicized Caribbean Basin Initiative (CBI) of President Reagan's government in the early 1980s, designed to provide the "carrot" of aid and so win friends for the US in the Caribbean, is but one indication of the priority given to the area. The extent of US influence in the region can be gauged by the example of tiny St Kitts and Nevis in 1983:

In recent years light component industries, mainly American-owned, have begun to sprout. But the islands are growing to depend upon tourism, for their really valuable asset is an astonishing beauty which American money, unchecked and uncontrolled, might purchase and so reduce them to a pair of floating Miamis.

Already Americans have bought from the Government the island's biggest hotel, and a new direct jet service to New York has been inaugurated. Last year the New York Times voted St. Kitts the best tourist resort visited and one of its hotels the best of the year. In the exclusive Frigate Bay Region, many new apartments and villas are being advertised in US dollars only. (*The Guardian*, London, September 16th 1983)

## YOUNG HISTORIAN

**A**

1 Using a detailed map of the Caribbean list each country, noting the country to which each has been historically linked. Include any changes that have occurred.
2 Why do hurricanes occur? Trace the direction hurricanes have followed in the Caribbean. Find out more about the effects of one hurricane in the Caribbean.
3 Write for information on tourism in the Caribbean. How does the information provided differ? What aspects of the Caribbean are stressed in the information?
4 Why has Cuba been seen as such a threat to the US since 1959?
5 List the products which have traditionally been associated with the Caribbean. Explain the changes in emphasis in exports from the Caribbean.

# THE COLONIAL HERITAGE

The influences that have shaped the Caribbean are so various, so diverse, as to be almost bewildering. In their time, the British, Spanish, French, Dutch, Danish and Swedes; more recently, North America, the United States and Canada, have all made their mark on the region.

## THE INDIGENOUS PEOPLE OF THE CARIBBEAN

Nor was the Caribbean uninhabited before Europe made contact and "discovered" it. The indigenous population of the Caribbean probably amounted to about three quarters of a million at the time of Columbus's discovery in 1492. Most lived on Hispaniola, probably half a million, with a further 50 thousand on Cuba, 20 thousand on Jamaica, with small or visiting populations on the other islands.

These people were the Ciboneys, the Guanahuatebeyes, the Taino Arawaks and the Caribs, who gave their name to the sea and to the region. The life led by the Arawaks, and the other Antillean people, appears to have been simple but more than adequate. Certainly, the standard of living enjoyed by them was superior to that of their "conquerors". Agriculture and fishing were rich enough to support the population.

The Arawaks disappeared within the first century of Spanish occupation of the New World, from the treatment received at Spanish hands and from unaccustomed diseases brought from Spain, as well as by absorption into the ranks of the Caribs.

The Arawaks left behind enough of their culture to contribute to the diversity of influences that now comprise the Caribbean culture. They passed on to the Spanish their expertise in agriculture, medicinal herbs, even housing skills. Tobacco, potatoes, peanuts, maize, beans and other crops cultivated by the Spanish were derived from the Arawaks. Certainly, too, Spanish men mated with Arawak women and thereby they contributed to the ethnic variety of the Caribbean. The language of the Spanish-speaking Caribbean contains many words passed on by the Arawak Indians.

The Caribs were the last to enter the Caribbean islands, but by 1500 they had all but displaced the Arawaks. They survived, where the others did not, because they kept away from Spanish settlements. However, by the time of the arrival of the English and the French, the Caribs had learnt much from the Spanish and had adapted their lives accordingly. They had become settled farmers, producing crops like sugar, oranges and bananas, brought by the Spanish. They were still sufficiently warlike, however, to be a considerable nuisance to the European colonizers of the seventeenth and eighteenth centuries. Yet they were doomed, and their way of life with it, from the moment of their first contact with the Spanish.

## SLAVERY

Even by the end of the sixteenth century the Spanish islands of the Caribbean were beginning to exhibit all the variations of people that

7

acquisition of slaves became of paramount importance to the Spanish throne. From 1518-1640 some 75,000 African slaves, 60% of the total Trans-Atlantic trade, had been shipped to the Spanish colonies. After 1640 the Spanish monopoly of supplies of slaves to the Caribbean had been broken by the English, the French and the Dutch, all of whom had established their own colonies in the Eastern Caribbean. From then, all the European countries occupying parts of the Caribbean vied with one another for a share of the slave market. As sugar was introduced to the region as a plantation crop, the demand for slaves increased. Sugar and slavery were synonomous.

The total number of slaves brought to the Americas as a whole was about 10 million. The islands of the Caribbean and the countries bordering the Caribbean Sea took half that number in the 350 years of the period of the slave trade. By the eighteenth century sugar, based on slavery, dominated the Caribbean economy. In 1770, 81% of exports from the British Caribbean consisted of sugar, rum and molasses; from the French Antilles the figure was 49%; by 1855 84% of Cuba's exports were sugar or sugar-products.

The same experiences were repeated

**4 Bartholomé de Las Casas, whose statue is on the outskirts of Trinidad in Cuba, drew the attention of the Spanish Crown to the atrocities committed against the Indians of the New World and consistently agitated on their behalf. Las Casas was made Protector of the Indians in 1516, but was unable to halt their elimination.**

characterize contemporary times. The twenty-four towns set up by the Spanish had a population of 7,500 whites, 22,150 Indians and a group of 56,000 Africans, mestizos and mullatos. Spanish-speaking Africans had accompanied the very first Spanish expeditions and by the start of the sixteenth century outnumbered the Spanish colonists. The Arawaks had been destroyed by the Spanish in their attempts to make them into slaves, the Caribs were too warlike, and so African slaves were the obvious answer. Their numbers increased from that time on, in response to the demand for labour to make the New World. The

8

**5 Each country that has had an association with the Caribbean has left indelible marks upon it. In Curacao the architecture shows a strong Dutch influence.**

throughout the Caribbean; colonization, slavery and monoculture – wounds which left scars visible in the modern Caribbean. Nor did the abolition of Caribbean slavery free its slaves. In place of the whip and sweat came the ordeal of free labour, where black slaves were thrown onto a labour market that had no demand for them. With Africa closed as a source of cheap labour and with his slaves discarded, the planter turned to India and Asia.

## ASIAN IMMIGRATION

Even before the abolition of Caribbean slavery, planters were advocating, for the most blatantly opportunistic reasons, the introduction on a large scale of "free" workers from India. This new wave of immigrants began in 1838 and ended only in 1924.

Between 1838 and 1917, 238,000 Indians were introduced into British Guiana; 145,000 into Trinidad; 21,500 into Jamaica; 39,000 to Guadeloupe; 34,400 to Suriname; 1,500 to St Vincent; 2,500 to Grenada. Nor was India the only source. Chinese contract labourers were put to work alongside African slaves and in the period 1847-71 over 100,000 Chinese labourers were

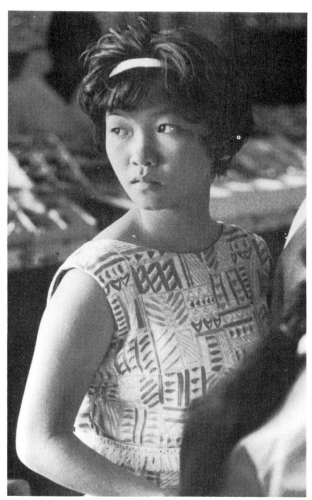

6 The population of Guyana reflects the African, Indian, Chinese, Portuguese and other European races who have played a part in its history.

brought to Cuba to work on the sugar estates. Such indentured labour from India and China in Cuba, Trinidad and Guiana made possible the growth of sugar production in the nineteenth century. The trade in Indian labourers ended only in 1917, at the express request of the Indian government.

By that time the further division between "coolie" and "nigger" had been added to the Caribbean society already groaning under the weight of racial and social strains. The antagonism between black and brown, African and Asian, is still a very obvious and negative element in Caribbean societies, especially in Trinidad and in Guyana. In Cuba, the Chinese population has all but been absorbed into society.

# RACE AND CLASS

Racial divisions in Caribbean society are the inevitable result of the racial organization of slavery. Black slaves were forcibly uprooted, taken away from their homeland, Africa, their very history and culture were denied them and they were forced into the mould of an alien life-style with an equally alien set of values. The modern descendants of African slaves are not unaware of the alien-ness of their position. Their position has been compared to that of the European Jew, uprooted by forces outside their control, at the mercy of accidental forces:

> Like the Jews, they have had unforgettable experiences. They have come through the wilderness, through a land of drought and of the shadow of death, through a land that no white man has passed through and where no white man has dwelt, and the misery and loneliness of it all is still with them. The more they evolve and the more they know, the more the heritage of race becomes a mystery, strange alike in its origin and in its intolerable pressure upon every moment of their lives. (W.P. Livingstone, *Black Jamaica,* London, 1899).

The racial division of society, and racialism itself, were daily reinforced through slavery. Even after emancipation, the spirit of slavery lingered on. The whites were fearful of a black uprising; the blacks, understandably, were mistrustful of their former masters. The system of values based on skin colour, apparent in today's Caribbean, was developed then as a defence. The divisions of society that went with racialism, and were further reinforced by the alien and divisive values associated with colonialism, held back the development of a national consciousness in most of the Caribbean, at the same time as they stimulated individualism and insularity. Puerto Rico and Cuba are, perhaps, the only exceptions.

In the first decades of the twentieth century, individual black people were allowed to rise in society to positions of responsibility, but this mobility was severely circumscribed. The pressures of the 1930s saw an acceleration of the rise of black people to responsible positions. Examinations for the Jamaican Civil Service were established in 1885 that allowed black people into so-called "white-collar" occupations. But the mass of society were unaffected by such tokens, their lot remained irredeemably miserable. At the same time as this "advancement" for black people was occurring, entry into "white society" was still rigidly controlled; in Cuba, until 1959, clubs, hotels, even beach resorts practised a colour bar. Even Batista, Cuba's President in the 1950s, was denied access to the most prestigious "white" club, because of his negroid appearance. In Jamaica the most important social occasions were restricted to "whites only". The Moyne Commission, sent to the British Caribbean in the wake of the disturbances of the 1930s, in 1939 noted that whilst racial prejudice was universally condemned by every witness who appeared before it, racialism was, nonetheless, on the increase.

# SYSTEMS OF GOVERNMENT

*The British Caribbean*
Each country in the British Caribbean, no matter what its size, had its own government from the moment of colonization. Each legislature was separate from every other, a jealously guarded preserve, and very expensive to run. Connected by trade with Britain and with other countries, but rarely with one another, the separate governments in each country served to reinforce the individualness of each, and this led on to the fragmentation of the region.

The political system in most British colonies was the representative system, made up of a Governor, a Council and an Assembly which did little more than represent the white minority, whose wealth was usually based upon sugar and slaves. The Governor was the Crown's representative and head of government, as well as being answerable to the local legislature. The Council was made up of members nominated by the Governor, who would normally be the rich and powerful. The Assembly was a representative body, though elected by a very narrow section of society which had a vote. In Trinidad, for example, the franchise was not increased until 1921; 17 years later only 6% of Trinidadians had the vote. In 1854 in St Vincent and St Lucia, respectively, there were only 193 and 166 registered voters, of whom 130 and 40 bothered to vote. In Tobago in 1862 two members were elected to the Assembly by one single illiterate voter.

The Assembly exercised considerable power, which brought it into confrontation with the Governor and the Colonial Office he represented. But although the representative system was discredited in the eyes of the Colonial Office, Parliament was not prepared to abolish it. When slavery was abolished, however, in 1834, a new system of government was called for which would preserve the existing status quo and deal with the potentially dangerous "problem" of giving political power to ex-slaves.

The first country to change was Jamaica, following the Morant Bay Rebellion of 1865. The Jamaican Assembly, led by the notorious Governor Eyre, under pressure from the Colonial Office and in the midst of riots, voted for its own abolition in 1866, and, after 200 years, was replaced with Crown Colony government which gave greater control to Britain. By the end of the nineteenth century the rest of the British Caribbean was governed by this system, with the exception of Barbados, Bermuda and the Bahamas, which retained their elected Assemblies. In British Guiana a semi-representative system was kept until 1928.

Crown Colony government is a system of rule by Governors appointed by the British Colonial Office. The Crown, therefore, has the power to dominate the colonial legislature, which could be a nominated one or partially elected. Crown Colony rule was preferred by the Colonial Office, as the old representative system had shown itself to be unstable and inefficient. Crown Colony government, in theory at least, opened the way to a much wider representation of society; and it also gave the Crown greater control of expenditure in its colonies. The new system would also bridge the divide between the poverty and ignorance of the black population and the selfishness and arrogance of the white minority.

Certainly, more harmonious relations existed between the different branches of the legislature under Crown Colony government than had existed before, making the enactment of legislation that much easier. In Jamaica, for example, 97 laws were passed in 1867 and 1868, under the leadership of Sir John Grant. Yet, by 1900,

dissatisfaction with Crown Colony rule was widespread in the Caribbean. Officials were forced by the system to vote against their own convictions, with unofficial members representing a united opposition. Nominated members were a source of friction in society, since they were not answerable to any electorate, nor were they swayed by public opinion. The mass of Caribbean people worked and paid taxes without any voice or influence in their own countries. The only way to air or redress grievances was through direct petition to the Colonial Office – a cumbersome procedure which was rarely successful. Self-government increasingly came to be seen as the only way to bring about the necessary economic and social changes that Crown Colony government was showing itself unable to provide. Discontent erupted in Trinidad in 1903, over the issue of the installation of water meters, though the reasons for the discontent were much more deeply rooted. Sixteen people were shot or bayoneted to death by police – vicious action that was subsequently deplored by a British enquiry.

After the First World War demands for self-government grew. Returning members of the West Indian Regiment, who had fought for European freedom and democracy, were in the forefront of demands for their own. West Indian lawyers, doctors, teachers and civil servants were emerging, despite the inadequate colonial models of education, demanding a say in the running of their countries' affairs.

In Grenada in 1914 T.A. Marryshow set up the Representative Government Association, which became the model for other British colonies in the Caribbean. A year later Marryshow established a newspaper, the title of which left no doubt of his views; called *The West Indian*, its influence was to spread throughout the region. Most British colonies had set up representative government associations by the 1920s, advocating a wider franchise, or constitutional reform or, like Marryshow's association, a federated West Indies.

As a response to internal demands, the Hon. E.F.L. Wood (later Lord Halifax) visited British Guiana and most of the other British colonies from December 1921 to January 1922. Wood believed that demands for self-government would eventually prove "irresistible", yet at the same time pleaded for caution. He considered that neither was there sufficient regional demand, at that time, to justify self-government, nor could it be granted in the near future. He recommended that the elective principle should be advanced gradually, in stages, seemingly unaware of the widespread desire for change or of the appallingly low level of West Indian political rights. In Jamaica, by far the most politically advanced country of the region, only 66,000 people, less than one twelfth of the population, had the vote; in Trinidad only 25,000 of a 400,000 population were eligible to vote. In such a context, demands for change would shortly take on a more dramatic form.

## The Hispanic Caribbean – Puerto-Rico

The nineteenth century witnessed Spain's decline in the New World which it had controlled for more than 300 years. All its colonies, with the exception of Cuba and Puerto Rico, were lost in the independence revolutions that swept through Latin America, or through sales, like that of Florida to the United States in 1821.

Both Cuba and Puerto Rico attempted to claim their independence in 1868; both were thwarted. The Puerto Rican "Grito de Lares", the call to independence from Lares, was quickly suppressed. In 1897 Spain did, however, grant Puerto Rico the right to elect its own legislature and to make its own laws, except those reserved by the Spanish Cortes. The right to send deputies to the Cortes in Madrid was also granted, as well as the right to establish commercial links with other countries. These were the very things that Puerto Ricans had demanded since 1868; their final granting came too late, for in December 1898 Puerto Rico was ceded to the United States at the Treaty of Paris ending the Spanish-Cuban-American War. From then, Puerto Rico was to remain under firm American control.

The country was occupied for two years until the Foraker Act established a civilian government, whose Governor, Cabinet and Judges were all US appointed. Economically, the island quickly moved towards US domination, with disastrous results for Puerto Ricans who found themselves strangers in their own country, displaced by North Americans. The Jones Act of 1917 gave Puerto Ricans their own Bill of Rights as well as US citizenship. In effect, the island had become a colony of the United States. Further, often radical and violent attempts to gain Puerto Rico's complete independence were extinguished when the leaders of the movement were imprisoned for conspiring against the United States.

Under the governorship of Luis Muñoz Marin – elected in 1948, 1952, 1956 and 1960 – Puerto Rico's economy showed dramatic improvements. Health, education and housing improved, per capita income rose from $121 in 1940 to $900 in 1965. Under Muñoz Marin the political status of Puerto Rico in relation to the US changed to that of *Estado Libre Asociado,* Associated Free State, giving Puerto Rico complete internal autonomy with continued US citizens' rights and rights to Federal services of the USA. The latter rights were especially important, for, despite the undoubted economic improvements, social and economic conditions remained poor for many Puerto Ricans, all of whom represent the poorest of all the US States. More than 50% of all Puerto Rican families receive Social Security benefits; in 1976 40% of all Puerto Ricans were unemployed.

## Cuba

Like Puerto Rico, Cuba entered the twentieth century under United States military occupation, the US having declared war against Spain in 1898. When the war ended nine months later, US troops remained in Cuba. The domination of the economy, society, politics and culture by the United States, which was to last until 1959, had begun. Earl T. Smith, American Ambassador to Cuba in the 1950s, summed up America's relationship with Cuba when he said that the US Ambassador to Cuba was always the second most important political figure in the country, sometimes *the* most important.

The nineteenth-century struggle for liberation and independence from Spain was thwarted by US intervention in the war with Spain, yet the ideas of freedom and liberation remained very much alive throughout the twentieth century. A revolutionary situation in Cuba in the 1930s was avoided largely through US interference in Cuban politics, leading to the emergence of Fulgencio Batista. The ideas and example of the nineteenth-century revolutionaries were taken up by Fidel Castro and his group in the 1950s, in their armed challenge to Batista that led to the Revolution, later to be transformed into a socialist revolution, which began in 1959.

7  American tourism to the Caribbean began at the start of the twentieth century. Panama hats were the attraction at Charlotte Amalia, capital of St Thomas, when it became US territory in 1915.

## YOUNG HISTORIAN

**A**

1  Find out more about the indigenous people of the Caribbean. What kind of lives did they lead? Were they warlike? Why have they all but disappeared?
2  What was Columbus's purpose in the Caribbean? Was he successful?
3  Were there differences in the way slaves were treated in the different Caribbean countries? Why did slavery persist in Cuba for longer than in the other countries?
4  What were the circumstances of the Morant Bay Rebellion in Jamaica in 1865? Write about Paul Bogle.
5  Why was Spain so anxious to hold onto Cuba and Puerto Rico in the nineteenth century?
6  What elements of "foreign" culture still exist in the Caribbean?

**B**

1  Imagine you are accompanying Columbus; describe your discovery of any one Caribbean island. Read Columbus's account of the discovery.
2  What would a typical day be like for a slave in the Caribbean? Write your account or speak it into a tape-recorder.

**C**

1  Compose newspaper headlines for (a) Columbus's discovery of the New World, (b) the abolition of slavery in the British Caribbean, (c) the Morant Bay Rebellion.
2  If you were able to interview Columbus, what ten questions would you ask him?

**D**

Design a poster *either* to attract Spaniards to the New World, *or* to commemorate the 500th Anniversary of Columbus's discovery.

# SLUMS OF EMPIRE

Many observers wrote of the distressing conditions in the Caribbean region as a whole at the start of the twentieth century. Lloyd George referred to the British West Indies as "slums of Empire"; Muñoz Marin, President of Puerto Rico, spoke of his own country as "a land of flattering statistics and distressing realities". He could all too easily have been speaking about the whole Caribbean.

**8   Men and women were used as beasts of burden in Caribbean ports until recent times, loading a variety of cargoes. Here coal is carried aboard ship in St Thomas, US Virgin Islands.**

## ROYAL COMMISSIONS

In the case of the British West Indies, Royal Commissions were appointed to examine and report on conditions whenever a situation appeared to be beyond the immediate control of the local Governor General and Administrators. In the late nineteenth and early twentieth centuries, there were numerous Commissions to the West Indies.

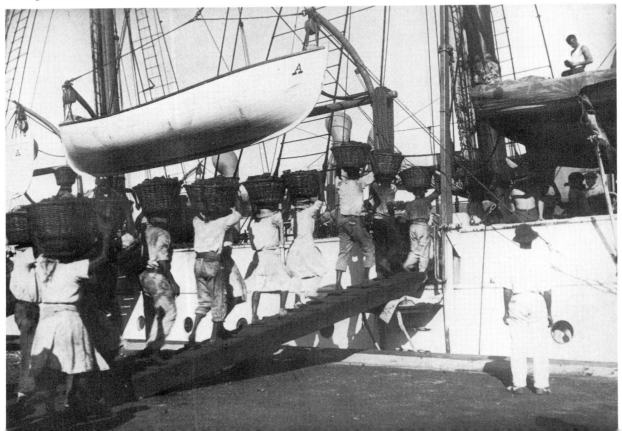

The 1897 Royal Commission was urgently constituted to examine the economic and social distress caused by the decline of West Indian sugar exports, in the face of competition from beet sugar, in the decade 1886-96, and the resulting fall by one fifth in wages of workers in the sugar industry. The Commissioners described conditions as "usually deplorable, sometimes desperate". The situation was so desperate that in 1898 the British Treasury lent Jamaica £100,000 solely to save the island from bankruptcy. Joseph Chamberlain, Secretary of State for the Colonies, made plain to Parliament the continuing responsibility of Great Britain to her Caribbean colonies. Grants would have to be made available lest the islands fall into social chaos and anarchy. The smaller islands, especially, faced difficulties, lacking even the barest resources to meet the cost of their administration. Grants, Chamberlain insisted, were the necessary expenses of Empire, not doles: "We cannot allow any part of the territory which we control and over whose finances we have complete authority to fall into anarchy and ruin."

The Commissioners were made aware of the depressingly negative effects of monoculture and they criticized the overemphasis on sugar that Britain had been responsible for establishing in the first place. They recommended diversification of agriculture into tropical fruits, as well as the development of technical and agricultural education. One of the major recommendations was to establish a small peasant class of farmers capable of responding to local demands, which would stimulate self-sufficiency and cut down on expensive imports. It was a view repeated vainly by other Commissions.

*The Royal Commission of 1930,* led by Lord Olivier, like that of 1897, was to look at the parlous state of the sugar industry. The price of sugar had been falling throughout the 1920s; in 1923 it stood at £23.10.00 a ton; by 1934 it had fallen to £5.00. Lord Olivier pointed to the high proportion of the West Indian population still employed in sugar, despite the warnings of the 1897 Commission, and to the catastrophe that would result from the complete decline of the industry. Olivier could do little more than repeat the earlier recommendations: the encouragement of alternative crops and employment, the extension of peasant ownership of the land, and the

9 **Joseph Chamberlain, Secretary of State for the Colonies from 1895-1903, was responsible for setting up the Norman Commission of 1896, to examine conditions in the British Caribbean**.

amelioration of the worst conditions of workers on the large estates. The position of the West Indian colonies as suppliers of cheap agricultural products was never questioned.

In the depressed conditions of the times, with high unemployment, low wages and increasing taxes, there were few avenues for the expression of discontent. Planters were unsympathetic to the establishment of trade unions and still few West Indians had the vote. In 1935 unemployed sugar workers on St Kitts showed their resentment by taking to the streets. In Trinidad the following year oil workers rioted, went on strike, then held hunger strikes. Jamaican dock workers and St Lucians working on coaling ships were the next to join the strikers. Strikes followed in all the British colonies. There had never been such widespread unrest in the area. Long-held grievances were being demonstrated for the first time.

A Commission of 1937, called to look into the disturbances emphasized the four areas of overpopulation, bad housing, unemployment and inadequate earnings as the causes. "No justification short of bankruptcy of trade and

15

industry" could be found for the appallingly low wages (an average of $1.78 weekly), and without a more equitable distribution of earnings between the employer and employed, the Commission contended, the great majority of workers would continue to feel bitterness and hatred. The creation of trade unions to represent workers' interests and the establishment of departments of labour in each country were recommended.

The "disturbances", as they were known in Westminster – the strikes, riots and labour revolts – resulted in injury, damage to property and loss of life. Criticism of the government's colonial policy, when these events were debated in the Houses of Parliament, resulted in the despatch of Major Orde Browne, labour advisor to the Secretary of State for the Colonies, to the West Indies to examine labour conditions. His Report (1939) was as depressing as those that had preceded it. He pointed to the succession of plant diseases that had devastated the area's crops, with consequent economic and social hardship. The problem of unemployment had been exacerbated by workers returning to their own countries after working on the building of the Panama Canal. Other countries in the area, like Cuba, which had hitherto taken in temporary workers, were themselves experiencing depressed conditions and had no need of extra labour. Even before the depression of the 1930s, the West Indian economies were in decline; the depression itself was the final insult.

Orde Browne recommended along the lines of his predecessors: the encouragement of independent farmers, so as to contribute to self-sufficiency and save on imports; but there was no certainty that this remedy, had it been followed, would have helped to solve the seemingly intractable problems. His observations on social conditions were damning: most West Indians, he found, although not hungry, were suffering from malnutrition; housing was deplorable, with overcrowding the norm in conditions lacking basic hygienic and sanitation facilities. Disease, inevitably, was rife: tuberculosis, malaria and venereal diseases were the most prevalent. Most families lived in great insecurity. The British colonies in the Caribbean, Orde Browne contended, needed trade union structures, labour legislation, workmen's compensation and arrangements for collective bargaining. Better and more medical care and greater opportunities for technical and agricultural education were other priorities.

The Orde Browne Report was important in that it influenced the Foreign Office in London, which thereafter actively encouraged labour legislation. Perhaps the most important value of his Report was the recognition that a more far-reaching investigation was long overdue. This was to be the purpose of the Moyne Commission.

*The Moyne Commission* Report, published fully in 1945, was the first of its kind to provide a comprehensive picture of British West Indian life and society. The Reports of 1897 and 1929-30 had been concerned with the sugar industry, and Orde Browne's with labour conditions.

> We feel justified in calling attention to the magnitude of the task which we attempted to fulfil in the last 15 months [1938-1939]. Few Royal Commissioners can ever have had to cover so wide a field of subjects . . . and few have had to cover so many scattered communities and conditions so diverse in spite of its apparent uniformity.

Their realization of the changed nature of the "West Indian Problem" was contained in the final section of their Historical Survey:

> Serious discontent was often widespread in the West Indian colonies during the 19th Century, as was indicated by the occasional uprisings that occurred, leading sometimes to considerable loss of life. But the discontent that underlies the disturbances of recent years is a phenomenon of a different character, representing no longer a mere blind protest against a worsening of conditions, but a positive demand for the creation of new conditions that will render possible a better and less restricted life. It is the co-existence of this new demand for better conditions with the unfavourable economic trend that is the crux of the West Indian problem of the present day.

The Report is a catalogue of the social and economic ills of the British Caribbean, and by implication an indictment of Britain's exploitation and then neglect of the area. It was especially an indictment of Crown Colony government.

The Moyne Commission Report contrasts sharply with the complacency and patronizing tone of Sir Sydney Armitage-Smith's observations in his 1931 Financial Report:

> A numerous, prosperous, happy and healthy peasant population, protected against plague, pestilence and

**10** The Moyne Commissioners in British Guiana (later Guyana) in January 1939. Lord Moyne, who led the Royal Commission, is second from the left. Their Report, finally published in 1945, was the first detailed investigation into Caribbean social and economic conditions.

famine, living in decent dwellings on holdings which, as the result of their own labour, wisely directed by Government, become their own property in their lifetime; [not influenced] by any harsh constraining law, but by the operation of their own unfettered choice, cherishing the land which offers to them generous nourishment, and enriching the Commonwealth by the fruit of their labours.

The picture painted by the Moyne Commissioners could hardly have been more different. Here there was no tropical paradise but hopeless and futureless conditions; a declining sugar industry on which a majority of the population depended, coupled with an exploitative cash work system of employment; wages so low that, as in the case of St Kitts and St Vincent, the rate had hardly moved above the rate of a shilling a day introduced at

emancipation in the nineteenth century; and malnutrition and widespread disease which a medical system, based upon cure rather than prevention, did little to contain and in some cases exacerbated. Housing brought to life Lloyd George's phrase, "slums of Empire"; rickety, insanitary, in which a variety of animal life co-existed with the human inhabitants. The opinion of the Commissioners on the results of West Indian education mirrored that of the West Indian Education Committee of 1931-32: if, wrote the Commissioners of the "lucky" West Indian child,

he has been fortunate enough to continue his education until school-leaving age, which is usually fourteen in the town and twelve in rural districts, he enters a world where unemployment and under-employment are regarded as the common lot. Should he find work as a manual labourer, his wages often provide only for bare maintenance and are far from sufficient to enable him to attain the standard of living which is set before him by new contacts with the outside world. If he is fitted by education and intelligence for clerical posts, competition for which is intense, he will have the prospect, at best, of a

17

salary on which, even in government employment he will find it a serious struggle to keep up the social position and appearances which he and his friends expect. He will have leisure hours but few facilities for recreation with which to fill them.

It is significant that this reference is in the masculine. The status of women in the Caribbean area generally at that time was extremely low. The Moyne Commissioners, for example, were able to discover only one woman who was a member of a West Indian Municipal Council.

The education system was described as "falling far short of any satisfactory standard", characterized, as it was, by absenteeism. Curricula had been copied from Britain, where they were now obsolete, and were irrelevant to West Indian needs. Teachers were employed "on the cheap", most of them being pupil teachers with little or no training. And school buildings were woefully inadequate to the task of education.

**11  A school in central Jamaica. Lack of educational provision together with curricula · ill-suited to the needs of Caribbean countries continue to hold back development in the area.**

To deal with the area's agrarian problems, which they identified as the main problem from which all others flowed, the Commissioners recommended a West Indian Welfare Fund to be financed by an Imperial Grant of £1 million per year for twenty years. This was to provide for the settlement of small farmers on the land, departments of labour throughout the region, welfare facilities and better housing, health and education provision. The ghosts of previous Commissions could be excused for remarking, "About time". The Orde Browne Commission had pressed for trade union and labour legislation, but, despite pressure for them in the previous ten years, the Moyne Commissioners could find no evidence of their existence.

It was because the Commissioners interpreted the basic problem of the West Indies as an agrarian one that they gave little consideration to industrial developments. This was but one of the weaknesses of the Report. Its great strength lay in the depth of its examination of British West Indian society; its weakness in the caution of its recommendations. What was required was an emphasis on economic development, to provide the

motor for change to break out of the established pattern of backwardness. The Commissioners chose to emphasize social welfare. The Colonial Development and Welfare Organization that emerged from the Moyne Commission Report showed all too clearly this thinking. That all the staff of the CDWO were English, despite the availability of numerous qualified West Indians, also showed that the British government intended to perpetuate its control over the West Indies.

Control was reinforced by the decision of the Commissioners not to recommend self-government based upon universal suffrage, though they all agreed that this should be the ultimate goal for the region. More participation, rather than self-government, was not likely to satisfy West Indian political demands. Nor was it only West Indians who found the system of Crown Colony government unacceptable. This is how Sir Stafford Cripps, barrister and leader of the left-wing of the British Labour Party, described the system in Jamaica in 1938:

> It means that if something exceptional occurs in Jamaica it may be that for one hour, or one hour and a half, during the course of twelve months a discussion will ensue and questions will be put in the House of Commons. During that period of time the Colonial Secretary will be armed with particulars from the Colonial Office obtained from the local government and he will courteously assure everyone that their facts must be wrong. And as he has the assurance that he is always right and as no vote of effectiveness can take place at the termination of the question, the interests of Jamaica will be put to bed for a further twelve months. And if you will add to this picture a true picture of the administration of colonial affairs of empire – the Parliamentary discussion of affairs – there will probably be present in the House of Commons not more than forty people, not half a dozen of them having the slightest knowledge of what they are talking about, you will appreciate that the Imperial Administration by the Imperial Parliament can hardly be looked upon as an effective or constructive method of managing colonial dependencies.

Although the Report was dismissed by some political parties in the West Indies as an attempt to introduce social services in place of needed political and economical reforms, it was, nonetheless, an important document that ushered in some changes, hastening the introduction of others. More than that, the process of the Commissioners in the different West Indian countries, soliciting opinions and discussion, helped to raise the growing political consciousness of the West Indians and gave a sense of identity and prestige to the people as a whole.

The full text of the Report was not published until 1945, though its recommendations were released in 1940, leading to the Colonial Development and Welfare Acts of the 1940s and '50s. The Colonial Development and Welfare Act of 1940 allocated £50 million annually over a ten-year period over the entire colonial network, not just the West Indies, with a further £500,000 for research. About one fifth was allocated for the British Caribbean.

The 1945 Act increased funds to £140 million, £15.5 million of which was earmarked for the British Caribbean. From 1940 to 1953 grants and loans from Colonial Development and Welfare funds amounted to £28 million, more than twice the amount recommended by Moyne. Despite the obvious benefits coming from much of the work of the CDWO, for many West Indians its work was found wanting. All CDWO projects were rurally biased and were piecemeal attempts to improve social welfare and agriculture rather than coming to grips with the long-established structural problems of the economy. Marryshow of Grenada spoke for many other West Indians when he remarked that he would have more faith in CDWO when he saw a West Indian on its executive.

## INVESTIGATIONS IN CUBA AND PUERTO RICO

In Puerto Rico a 1939 investigation of 6,000 families with over 34,000 of their members in the coffee, fruit and tobacco regions revealed that they received an average daily rate of just 60 cents. 60% of the farm-workers studied earned an average annual income of less than $100; the remaining 40% earned less than $150. In 1934 Puerto Rican needleworkers earned 12½ cents an hour; homeworkers earned just 4 cents. 65,000 persons were employed in the Puerto Rican needlework industry at that time.

Sugar, as in the rest of the Caribbean, dominated the Puerto Rican agricultural economy. During the *zafra,* the sugar cane harvest, from January until June, employment is plentiful; in-between is the "tiempo muerto", the dead season, when the industry has no need of workers. Mechanization added to the problem in Puerto Rico, reducing the demand for labour even more. A study of working conditions in the sugar industry showed that labourers in sugar cane planting worked an average of 34 weeks a year; only 10% of unskilled workers and 40% of skilled workers worked the whole year.

Nor were workers in other agricultural sectors any better-off. But sugar was the most important sector of the economy, with its defenders claiming natural advantages to the production of that one crop. One acre of sugar, it was claimed, would purchase the product of five acres of coffee; four of sweet potatoes, or yams, or white potatoes; six acres of dried beans; nine acres of pigeon peas or rice; twenty-one and a half of corn. It was argued that export crops like sugar yielded higher incomes per acre than crops for the home market.

**12 New technology is rapidly replacing traditional ways of cane-cutting in the modern Cuban sugar industry.**

These higher incomes, as we have already seen, were not being enjoyed by Puerto Rico's agricultural workers. A study of one Puerto Rican town showed a daily expenditure on food for a family of six of 23 cents. A rural labourer had an income of 12 cents a day and nearly 80% of earnings in rural areas was spent on food simply for subsistence.

That most Puerto Ricans were on a deficient diet was an inescapable reality borne out by the measurement of 15,500 agricultural labourers. They were shorter and weighed less than comparable US army recruits or US adults. Most were found to be suffering from disease.

In Haiti, an investigation of 884 rural families in 1938 showed that 15% ate only one meal a day, 45% ate twice a day. Those fortunate enough to eat three times a day made do with a piece of boiled banana or cassava for at least one of those meals. Some families did not eat meat for two or three months. Haitian soldiers received 15 cents a day for food; a prisoner 10 cents.

A United States Commission sent to Cuba in 1935, under the auspices of the Foreign Policy Association, found that the annual cost of food

necessary to sustain an adult male was $38 – far in excess of the resources of most workers. The Report captured well the tyranny of sugar in Cuba. It could have been describing any other sugar producer in the Caribbean:

> With the sugar crop, activity commences over the island. Families begin to purchase meat and rice to build up the terrific energy which must be expended in the field. Clothing and shoes are bought . . . Lights appear about the countryside as the families once more have enough money to buy kerosene . . . . During a normal season everything quickly assumes the air of prosperity. But after two to five months of steady employment the atmosphere begins to change . . . the cane families begin to reduce their expenditure because they can see the dead season ahead. Each worker is willing to take a lower paid job if he can only have something to do for money. Store-keepers reduce the stocks of goods on their shelves and the travelling salesmen retire to Havana. Gradually the prosperity of the *zafra* passes away and the kerosene lamps in the *bohios* begin to flicker out. Meat, rice with lard, and beans, which have been the foundations of the *zafra* diet now come fewer times each week. The cane cutter looks about him for substitute foods, turning to plantains, sweet potatoes, malanga, and yucca. Instead of drinking coffee, he begins to depend on cane juice which he manufactures by a crude hand press in his doorway. Gradually, the people reduce their diet. The masses, who do little or no planting of their own, beg and pick up food as best they can or migrate elsewhere for work if such can be found. The rains begin and with them comes malaria. Yet there is no money for doctors or medicine.

In its *Report on Cuba* in 1950 the World Bank repeated the depressing picture of the 1930s. Sugar still dominated the economy and society to the virtual detriment of everything else. The economy had stagnated because of the sugar monoculture and the close, unhealthy economic and political relationship with the United States. From the 1920s to the 1950s Cuba showed little progress. In some areas even, like education, the situation had worsened; proportionately fewer school-age children were in school in the 1950s than had been the case in the 1920s. A survey of 1,000 cases in 1956 showed a per capita income of $91.25; more than two thirds of expenditure went on food; almost a quarter (24%) of the diet was rice with beans and root crops; only 11% of families' diet included milk; 4% meat; 2% eggs; 1% fish. Green vegetables were never mentioned.

Health standards were appalling. More than one third interviewed had intestinal parasites; 13% were suffering or had suffered from paludism and 14% from tuberculosis; 13% had had typhus. Almost nine tenths of Cuban peasants had to pay for medical care out of earnings. Government subsidies were only 8% of medical services on offer. 70% of families had no medicines in their houses.

53% of those interviewed could read and write; 4% could read but not write; the rest – 43% – were totally illiterate. 44% had never entered school; of those who had, 88% had not progressed beyond third grade – not even Elementary level.

Yet Cuba was seen as one of the richer Caribbean countries. The land may have been rich, as elsewhere; the people were poor.

## YOUNG HISTORIAN

**A**

1 List the most important investigations into Caribbean conditions. What was their purpose? Did they yield results?
2 Why was the Moyne Commission so different from other Royal Commissions?
3 Should Spain, Britain or the United States accept "responsibility" for conditions in the Caribbean?
4 Find out more about Joseph Chamberlain's period in office as Secretary of State for the Colonies.
5 Why has sugar beet been grown in Europe at the expense of cane grown in the Caribbean?

**B**

1 You are investigating conditions in the Caribbean. (a) Where would you want to go? (b) What would you want to see? (c) How would you explain the apparent indifference of Britain, and other countries, to the conditions?

**C**

You are a sugar-cane worker in the Caribbean. How does your life change throughout the year?

**D**

Make a poster to draw attention to poor conditions in *either* Health *or* Education *or* Employment in the Caribbean.

# SOCIAL AND POLITICAL UNREST

The twentieth century opened with no Caribbean country truly independent. Cuba and Puerto Rico were virtually US colonies; Haiti and the Dominican Republic were under the ever-watchful eye of the American eagle. Jamaica, Trinidad, Barbados, Guiana and the smaller Eastern Caribbean islands were part of the British Empire. Aruba, Bonaire, Curacao and Suriname on the Latin American mainland belonged to Holland. The French possessed Guadeloupe and Martinique, with French Guyana on the mainland. The Danish owned the Virgin Islands until 1915, when they were sold to the United States.

In Puerto Rico and Cuba a strong sense of nationalism was already well-developed and had led to struggles for independence. In the British West Indies a sense of nationalism or even class-consciousness was slow to emerge.

## THE BRITISH WEST INDIES

A number of factors came together to bring about a period of unrest in the British Caribbean that resulted in reforms to colonial rule and ultimately in Britain's retreat from the area. Widespread unrest was preceded by the rise of individual West Indian radical leaders such as Sandy Cox and J.A.G. Smith in Jamaica and A.A. Cipriani in Trinidad. West Indians who had fought in the First World War returned home changed by the experience, willing to press for change. Economic conditions in the inter-war years, especially the

13 The War Memorial in Bridgetown, Barbados, for those West Indians who died fighting alongside the Allies in World War One. It was the experience of war that contributed to demands for self-government throughout the Caribbean.

22

crisis in Caribbean sugar, caused acute personal hardship, especially in the rural areas where people's lives had changed little since emancipation. Already bad conditions worsened. Emigration to Cuba, Panama and the United States was closed, so cutting off one safety-valve. Black consciousness was raised, too, by those like Marcus Garvey, who brought the experience of black people of the United States to the Caribbean through his United Negro Improvement Association. All served to reinforce deep-seated resentment and discontents. Social and political upheaval were inevitable.

---

## MARCUS GARVEY

---

"Two black West Indians using the ink of negritude wrote their names imperishably on the front pages of the history of our time. Standing at the head is Marcus Garvey," wrote C.L.R. James in his book on the Haitian slave rebellion, *The Black Jacobins*. He was echoing many who see Marcus Garvey as having made a fundamental contribution to the sense of racial consciousness, and racial pride, of black people in the Caribbean and throughout the world.

Garvey's original contribution was to create a movement, based upon race, the United Negro Improvement Association (UNIA), which, due to Garvey's exceptional talents as an organizer, was to penetrate every corner of the earth.

Garvey's parents were poor peasants who lived on the north coast of Jamaica; in his early years he came to know hunger and deprivation as a daily reality. The bitter lessons of racial discrimination he learned as a child. From 1909 to 1911 Garvey travelled throughout Central America where, along with the thousands of other West Indian migrant workers building the Panama Canal, or working in mines or in agriculture, he experienced even more the indignities of racialism. In 1912 he travelled to London, where he was able to develop further his ideas about the position of black people in society. He studied in London and came into contact with Pan-Africanists. After reading *Up From Slavery*, by the American negro leader, Booker T. Washington, Garvey thought of becoming a leader of his people.

I asked myself, "Where is the black man's government?", "Where is his King and his kingdom?", "Where is his President, and his Ambassador, his army, his navy, his men of big affairs?". I could not find them, and then I declared, "I will help to make them . . . I saw before me then . . . a new world of black men, not peones, serfs, dogs, and slaves, but a nation of sturdy men making their impress upon civilisation and causing a new light to dawn upon the human race. I could not remain in London any more.

Returning to Jamaica in 1914, he had, within five days of his arrival, organized the UNIA to unite "all the negro peoples of the world into one great body to establish a country and government absolutely their own". UNIA's motto was, "One God. One Aim. One Destiny."

Garvey corresponded with Booker T. Washington in the United States about the establishment of colleges for Jamaican negroes like those Washington had founded in the USA. In

**14** Marcus Garvey, persecuted in his own time, is now a hero in his own country, Jamaica, as well as in many African countries whose independence he inspired.

ONE GOD

ONE AIM

ONE DESTINY

MARCUS GARVEY

spite of Washington's death, Garvey went ahead with his plans to visit the US. Finding the same racialism there that he had encountered in the Caribbean, Central America and in London, he set up a branch of the UNIA in New York. Within three months 2,000 members were enlisted. By 1919 there were 30 branches in different cities of the United States, with a membership of over 2 million. Garvey had also begun to publish a newspaper, *The Negro World,* to give further circulation to his ideas. Not all countries welcomed the newspaper; in French Dahomey possession of it could lead to life imprisonment. In 1919 Garvey established a steamship company, the Black Star line, which would form a link between the black peoples of the world. The ships were bought at over-rated prices; the line incompetently run. In 1922 the company went out of business and paved the way for Garvey's downfall in the United States.

By 1923 much opposition had grown towards Garvey in the US. Many black intellectuals had opposed him from the beginning, others came to oppose him through their membership of rival black organizations. They were joined by the American white establishment. Garvey was tried and convicted of "using the US mails to defraud" by using the mails to promote the sales of shares in the Black Star line. Freed on bail pending appeal, Garvey went ahead undaunted to establish another shipping line and with plans to settle American negroes in Liberia.

When, in 1925, his appeal was dismissed, Garvey began a five-year prison sentence. Released after serving three years, he was deported to Jamaica where he immediately began political agitation. He formed his own political party, the People's Political Party, in 1929, based upon a manifesto that was way ahead of its time. His ideas were more in line with modern times than the 1920s and he was able to make little inroad into Jamaican politics. Dispirited, Garvey left Jamaica in 1935 for exile in London. In 1940, penniless and friendless, he died of a stroke.

Disregarded in his own time, Garvey was subsequently celebrated in his own country, when, in 1964, his body was repatriated and he was reburied as a "Hero of Jamaica". Many African leaders have paid tribute to the influence of Garvey's ideas on them and their people. The

Ghanaian government named its shipping line the Black Star Line, after Garvey. In the Caribbean, Garvey's influence is unquestionable through his philosophy to "teach the black man to see beauty in himself".

## THE DISTURBANCES

From the end of the First World War to the end of the 1920s, discontent led to riots throughout the British Caribbean. Although these riots took the form of labour agitation, the reasons for them lay in the wider political and social context already mentioned. In the period 1935 to 1938 the British Caribbean, to the consternation of the British government, was set alight with strikes, riots and unrest. In 1935 the sugar workers of St Kitts and British Guiana struck, followed by a coal strike in St Lucia and a strike against increased customs duties in St Vincent. In 1937 the oilfield workers in Trinidad went on strike, giving the lead to a general strike. Similar unrest spread to Barbados, St Lucia, British Guiana and Jamaica. Jamaican dock workers refused to work without better pay and conditions of work. The reasons for all these strikes were clearly based upon local conditions and grievances, but the root cause of the general upheaval lay in the nature of colonial society itself, as the Moyne Commission was later to accept.

The response of the Crown was to rush military reinforcements to the Caribbean to back-up the hard-pressed police unable to cope with these unforeseen violent events. Should they have been foreseen?

Local order was finally restored by Britain, but the cost had been high: 29 dead, 115 wounded and considerable damage to property. The experience was to change definitively the political make-up of the British Caribbean and hasten Britain's decolonization of the area.

## TRADE UNIONS AND POLITICAL PARTIES

The "disturbances" in the British Caribbean took

place not only in a context of grinding poverty reinforced by the world slump but also where trade unions did not exist because of employers' opposition, where there was no machinery for collective bargaining, and where only a handful of the population had the vote. It should come as no surprise, then, that out of the discontent and resentments of the 1930s came labour movements, and from them political parties and clearly identifiable political leaders.

In Trinidad and Tobago the trade union and political developments of the 1930s were inextricably linked to the activities of two men, Arthur Cipriani and Uriah "Buzz" Butler. Cipriani had fought in the First World War in the West Indian contingent and was one of many to take to political agitation on his return. He was one of the unofficial members of Trinidad's Legislative Council, sat on the Port of Spain Council for fifteen years from 1926-41 and was elected Mayor of Port of Spain no fewer than eight times. He was a vocal critic of the British government and pressed for representative government not only as a member of the "opposition" in the Legislative Council but also through his newspaper, *The Socialist*. Cipriani took on the interests of Trinidad's working class by re-organizing the Trinidad Working Men's Association, later renamed the Trinidad Labour Party, in 1932. He agitated for old age pensions, minimum wages and for local control over utilities like electricity and telephones. By 1938 the Trinidad Labour Party (TLP) had 120,000 members representing a third of Trinidad's population. Significantly, Cipriani had been able to attract both black and East Indian workers, despite the overt racial tensions between these two groups. The violence of the 1930s was not at all to Cipriani's taste, having put his trust in the constitutional road by pressing for reforms with the help of the British Labour Party.

Cipriani's political career declined with the rise of other, more militant leaders who were more at home in the confrontational atmosphere of the time. He was finally defeated by a combination of the imperial enemy and the hostility of fellow Trinidadians. It could also be said that he was his own worst enemy because of his dependence on and trust in the British Labour Party, his own vague political position which ill-equipped him to

**15** Uriah, "Buzz", Butler on his arrival in London for a visit in the 1950s.

deal with the immediacy of the changing political events of the 1930s, and his insistence on fighting for self-determination for Trinidad within a constitutional framework.

"Buzz" Butler came to the attention of the people in 1935, when he led the unemployed on a hunger march. The next year, expelled from the TLP, he set up the British Empire Workers' and Citizens' Home Rule Party. In June 1937 Butler called a sit-down strike in the Trinidadian oil-fields, which led to violence with the police. Despite a $500 reward for information of Butler's hiding-place, he was not arrested and eventually gave himself up on the promise of a fair trial. Butler's demands were for higher wages and for changes in the political system which gave the vote to only 7% of the population. "Buzz" Butler was the first black political leader to emerge in Trinidad.

When the Second World War broke out, Butler was interned, though without charges being laid against him or going to trial. He was simply regarded as a threat to the State. Released in 1945, he set up his party to contest the 1946 election.

Trade unions proliferated in Trinidad following the 1937 unrest; the oil workers, sugar workers, seamen and dock workers, clerical workers and shipwrights all became represented by newly developed trade unions. The oil workers' and sugar workers' unions went on to form two general unions, the Transport and General Workers' Union and the Federated Workers' Union. This experience was mirrored elsewhere in the Caribbean.

In Jamaica trade unions were organized in the docks and amongst cigar workers and industrial workers after the First World War, but they remained hamstrung by a lack of adequate legal protection. In 1935 the main union was the Jamaican Workers' and Tradesmen's Union that had been founded by A.G.S. "Father" Coombs and Alexander Bustamante, who was to play a crucial role in the labour and political development in Jamaica. Bustamante, just like Butler in Trinidad, gained a reputation as a radical through his imprisonment on a charge of incitement and sedition during the disturbances of the 1930s. Bustamante's cousin, Norman Manley, himself to play an important part in the union and political life of Jamaica – took up Bustamante's cause:

> I give up my law practice [he was a KC and leading barrister in Jamaica] to take into my hands the case of the people of Jamaica before the bar of history, against poverty and need – the case of my country for a better life and freedom in our land.

For the next thirty years Bustamante and Manley were to dominate Jamaican politics. Yet they could not have been more different. Manley was an urbane, cultivated, professional man of complete integrity; Bustamante a flamboyant street politician who revelled in describing himself as having "been raised in the gutter". Sir Grantley Adams, another accomplished political leader to emerge during this period, said:

> Manley is a statesman who will never be a politician. Bustamante is a politician who will never be a statesman.

In May 1938 the Bustamante Industrial Trade Union (BITU) was formed, with Bustamante at its head. The BITU was a general union which attracted skilled as well as unskilled workers, black as well as East Indian. Bustamante explained his motives, and ambitions, to the Jamaican *Daily Gleaner* in an interview on 31 August 1938:

> Yes, I want power, sufficient power to defend those weaker than I am; those less fortunate, and that's what I have today, power. It has been stated that I want to be a dictator. Yes, I do want to dictate the policy of the unions in the interests of the people I represent, and the only ones who are giving results today are the dictators . . . the voice of labour must be heard and it shall be heard through me.

In September 1938 Manley founded the People's National Party (PNP), announcing his support for adult suffrage, economic and social reform, trade unionism and eventual independence from Britain. Manley also gave his support for a West Indian Federation, for which enthusiasm had been growing, especially in the Eastern Caribbean.

Although Bustamante's union, the BITU, supported the formation of Manley's PNP, it was not to be long before the two men were to take separate political careers. In February 1942, Bustamante, after a further 17 months in prison, took command of a union that had been reinvigorated largely by the efforts of Manley, only to publicly break with him later to form his own party, the Jamaican Labour Party (JLP). The

JLP was to be the political arm of Bustamante's union, in opposition to Manley's predominantly middle-class PNP, now without union support. The two-party system in Jamaica was the first to emerge in the British Caribbean, though the charismatic personalities of the two men were to remain more important than the structures of the parties themselves.

The other British Caribbean islands were to see similar developments: labour disturbances leading to the formation of trade unions, political parties and the emergence of credible political leaders. On St Kitts the St Kitts-Nevis Trade and Labour Union was formed in 1940, with Paul Southwell and Robert Bradshaw emerging out of the organization to form political parties. In St Vincent a Labour Party was founded after the development of the St Vincent Working Class Association in 1935. Similarly, in St Lucia the St Lucia Workers' Cooperative led to the St Lucia Labour Party.

In Barbados, Grantley Adams, later Sir Grantley Adams, emerged as the island's leader. Adams was a black middle-class lawyer who came

to prominence as the defence lawyer at the trial of Clement Payne, "Buzz" Butler's Minister of Propaganda, who had gone to Barbados as a political agitator. In 1938 Adams founded the Barbados Progressive League, from which was to come the Barbados Workers' Union, in 1941, and the Barbados Labour Party.

## HAITI, THE DOMINICAN REPUBLIC AND CUBA

The non-British Caribbean experienced its own brand of economic distress and unrest in the first quarter of the twentieth century. In Cuba, Haiti and the Dominican Republic the United States had consistently used the policy of military intervention and occupation, unlike the softer approach of the British. Haiti was occupied by more than two thousand US Marines from 1915-34

**16 The Jamaican "disturbances". Alexander Bustamante, Jamaican trade union leader, pleads for restraint from striking Jamaican workers.**

to "maintain order, to provide an atmosphere conducive to American investment and to construct basic public works". To that end, the Marines built roads, schools and hospitals and installed telephone and telegraph cables, yet they made no attempt to contribute to the development of Haitian political institutions, or to raise the levels of administrative or educational standards. US Marines left Haiti in 1934, in line with the then President Roosevelt's stated policy to create a "Good Neighbour Policy" in the region. Haiti's economy and politics degenerated with the withdrawal of the US Marines and took on the characteristics of poverty, disease, malnutrition and corruption that have since dogged the country.

The Dominican Republic, next to Haiti, had a similar experience and relationship with the USA. Military occupation from 1916 to 1924 resulted, as in Haiti and Cuba, in the construction of roads and bridges, schools and hospitals, sanitation and communication, but contributed nothing towards the Dominicans being able to govern their own affairs. The depression years ushered in three decades of dictatorial rule by Trujillo, supported by the USA until his violent assassination in 1961. Rafael Leonides Trujillo took power in a coup in

**17 Troops move in on demonstrators in Port-au-Prince, Haiti on Election Day 1946. The use of force and coercion has been a consistent part of political life from that time.**

1930, after which he systematically took personal control of the police and armed forces, the government and the judiciary, as well as the day-to-day running of the Dominican economy. With his family and friends, Trujillo owned 75% of the Dominican economy, controlling milk and meat monopolies, rice, potatoes, oils and sugar. On his death he was said to own 1,500,000 acres of cultivated land; his factories employed 60,000 workers. The total value of his possessions in the Dominican Republic and abroad has been calculated at over $500 million. Trujillo kept himself in power through one of the most vicious tyrannies ever experienced in the Caribbean. Yet he was condoned and supported by the USA. As President Roosevelt was to say: "He may be a son of a bitch, but he is *our* son of a bitch".

For Cuba, the twentieth century began under US occupation. Cuba had gained its nominal independence in 1898, at the close of the Spanish-Cuban-American war, but at the same time US occupation began. Further salt was to be rubbed into the wound by the United States who chose the first Cuban President, wrote the first Cuban constitution and imposed upon this newly "independent" island the Platt Amendment in 1901, which gave the US the right to intervene in Cuba's international policy-making, and in the running of its economy, and a natural harbour for a marine base which is still occupied in 1984.

**18** The car in which President Rafael Trujillo, the hated dictator of the Dominican Republic, met his death in 1961.

The price of sugar dictated the economic fortunes of Cuba, just as it did in the rest of the Caribbean. Cuba became increasingly dependent on this one crop. In 1909 sugar accounted for 54% of Cuba's exports; by 1918, 89%. The ending of the First World War was to have a dramatic effect on Cuban sugar fortunes. The entire 1918-19 sugar crop had been bought in advance by the newly-formed Sugar Equalization Board in the US, which subsequently sold it for a $42 million profit. In response to the angry protests of Cuban sugar producers, the next year's crop was put on the world market free of controls. What followed has become known as "The Dance of the Millions". Sugar which fetched 5½ cents a pound at the end of the war rose to 20 cents a pound by May 1920. The high price was short-lived, based as it was on speculation and an imaginary sugar shortage. By October the price had fallen to 7 cents a pound and continued to fall. Banks, which had lent money on anything remotely associated with sugar, were forced to close their doors. Much of Cuba's sugar industry fell into the hands of American interests through foreclosures that reinforced the "Americanization" of Cuba that had begun with the first occupying US troops. By the *zafra* of 1926-27 more than 62% of Cuban sugar was produced in US-owned sugar mills with some $600 million invested in Cuban sugar alone.

With US control of the main sector of the Cuban economy went political control. A US Ambassador to Cuba once boasted that anyone occupying his position in Cuba was almost the second most important politician, sometimes *the* most important. This was to be borne out by the events of the 1930s.

Cuban-US relations began badly with the imposition of the Hawley-Smoot tariff which imposed high duties on Cuban sugar and other exports to the US, though these were subsequently lowered in 1934. The US had tolerated the repressive regime of Gerardo Machado from 1925-33 and they made sure that the revolutionary government that followed Machado could not succeed, through outright interference in Cuba's internal politics and through an indirect show of force by parading the US fleet off the Cuban coast. The result was the emergence of Fulgencio Batista as Cuba's new "strong-man" in 1933, a position he occupied until his flight from Cuba on New Year's eve, 1958.

## YOUNG HISTORIAN

**A**
1 Why was Marcus Garvey not appreciated in his own lifetime?
2 How and why did the "disturbances" in the British Caribbean affect every country?
3 Are there special reasons why trade unions led to wider political organization in the Caribbean?
4 How did the world economic crisis of the 1920s and '30s affect the Caribbean?
5 Did the attitude of the US Government towards the Caribbean change in the 1930s? What was "The Good Neighbour Policy"?
6 How did the Second World War change (a) Britain's and (b) the United States's position in the Caribbean? What did the Second World War change in the Caribbean itself?

**B**
1 You are in one of the Caribbean islands during the "disturbances" of the 1930s. Write an account of what you see and hear.
2 You are a journalist sent to Haiti in 1915 to cover the US Marine landings. Describe the conditions you find on your arrival.

**C**
1 Write headlines to announce (a) the occupation of Haiti by the US, (b) the labour unrest in the British Caribbean, (c) the trial of Marcus Garvey in the US, (d) the end of the "Dance of the Millions" in Cuba.

**D**

Design posters (a) for a meeting of Marcus Garvey's UNIA and (b) to recruit members to a new Caribbean trade union.

# ATTEMPTS AT CO-OPERATION

The reason for the notorious isolationism of Caribbean countries does not lie only in the geography of the region. The distances between the countries are not great, nor are there insurmountable natural obstacles to be overcome. The non-physical barriers of language, custom and culture appear to be greater obstacles to unity and co-operation. There are historical factors that are still potent forces in the Caribbean: the three hundred years of British rule, for example, which kept the islands apart, preferring to emphasize the individual link between each island and the metropolis. The same could be said of the French colonies, the Dutch with theirs, or the United States with Puerto Rico. Yet the future of the Caribbean lies in co-operation and developing a sense of communal identity.

The obvious economic and political advantages to unity and co-operation, which in the case of the smaller islands, could be their very salvation, have long been recognized. The problems of the short-lived Federation of the West Indies, from 1958-62, and the history of CARICOM, illustrate the nature of the difficulty of co-operation amongst Caribbean neighbours.

## THE CARIBBEAN COMMISSION

The Caribbean Commission, although a special case during wartime, was an early attempt at co-operation in the region. The Anglo-Caribbean Commission was established in 1942, to bring about co-operation between the United States and Britain in the area of the Caribbean. In 1940 Britain obtained 50 obsolete American destroyers from the US, in return for 99-year leases of land for air and sea bases in the Bahamas, Jamaica, British Guiana, Trinidad, St Lucia, Antigua, as well as in Newfoundland and Bermuda. This move represented a further and dramatic advance by the US into the Caribbean, and signalled a further retreat by Britain. West Indians generally resented bitterly this intrusion by the Americans, though the work provided at US bases was welcome. The resentment was especially felt in Trinidad, whilst in St Lucia sugar and banana plantations suffered a labour shortage because workers were drawn to better jobs on the US base.

In 1945 France and Holland, both with interests in the Caribbean, joined the Commission and its name changed simply to the Caribbean Commission, with its headquarters in Port of Spain, Trinidad. A positive step was the inclusion in the Commission of Caribbean representatives rather than, as hitherto, just British and Americans. The Commission met both frequently and regularly, publishing research and discussion papers on education, labour, health, welfare and housing. It established the Caribbean Medical Centre in Trinidad, and encouraged developments in tourism and agriculture. The value of the Commission was its emphasis on a regional approach to common problems.

The Commission was attacked for its high administrative costs and lack of concrete results. In 1961 it was replaced by the Caribbean Organization, with similar aims to the Commission. This time, however, the British, Americans, French and Dutch were simply observers, rather than active members. The Caribbean Organization, like its predecessor, was advisory rather than executive, and was described by Muñoz Marin of Puerto Rico as a "clearing house for ideas". The organization ceased to exist in 1965, when Puerto Rico, Suriname and British Guiana withdrew their support. Trinidad and Tobago, on independence a few years earlier, had already left. The collapse of the organization, like that of the Federation of the West Indies, illustrates some of the obstacles to co-operation amongst the countries of the Caribbean.

## MOVES TOWARDS FEDERATION IN THE BRITISH CARIBBEAN

The idea of a Federation was not new. For almost three centuries, from the start of Britain's involvement in the Caribbean, forms of association had been mooted to deal with the problems of administering the colonies, though the main enthusiasm came, not from West Indians, but from the British themselves. Throughout the nineteenth century enthusiasm for federation grew in the Colonial Office, but it was not until the 1940s that West Indians began to join in the enthusiasm. Perhaps the reason for their late conversion to the idea is that the term "federation" had different meanings for those using it. For some it invoked a general notion of "unity", for others federation meant self-determination and dominion status. For Cipriani, for example, with his leaning towards trade unionism, federation was the means by which social problems could be dealt with in a way of which Crown Colony government had shown itself to be incapable. For the Colonial Office, by contrast, federation was seen as a way of achieving economic and administrative efficiency; savings, even. West Indians were understandably suspicious that the Colonial Office was using the idea to extricate itself from its obligations to the region. Sharp differences of opinion, anyway, divided the British Caribbean. Most trade unions and political parties saw little gain in federation; individual politicians, fearful of losing power and prestige so newly acquired, were unlikely to be ecstatic about the possibility. There were exceptions: Marryshow of Grenada, Cecil Rawle of Dominica and Arthur Cipriani of Trinidad all

favoured federation. Marryshow went so far as to demand a Royal Commission to look at the possibility of both federation and self-government for the British West Indies.

In 1931 Lord Passfield, the Colonial Secretary, informed the Governors of Trinidad, the Windwards and the Leeward Islands of his intention to set up a Commission to examine possibilities for co-operation. A Closer Union Commission, arising out of this commitment, visited the Eastern Caribbean from November 1932-February 1933. Its Report showed the deep divisions which existed between the different islands, even those that were linked administratively as one. The Moyne Commissioners discovered a growing demand for closer union or forms of co-operation. Almost every witness interviewed was in favour of some form of federation, and this feeling was increasingly shared by the emerging trades union movement. Support, too, came from West Indians educated abroad. Among them was Dr Eric Williams, later to become Prime Minister of Trinidad/Tobago. Federation, he contended, should be sought, "not only by economic consideration but by every dictate of common sense". Further, an economic union of all the Caribbean – British, French, Dutch, American – should be the ultimate goal: "The Caribbean, like the whole world, will either federate or collapse." His comments are worth bearing in mind against his later actions.

The Caribbean Labour Congress, meeting in Barbados in September 1945, was a significant occasion, as it brought together the most important trade union and political leaders: Grantley Adams of Barbados, Hubert Critchlow of British Guiana, Richard Hart of Jamaica, representing the PNP, as well as St Kitts, T. Albert Marryshow of Grenada and Albert Gomes of Trinidad. There was no representative from Bustamante's ruling Jamaica Labour Party, because of his bad relations with the Eastern Caribbean governments. It was an ill omen for future developments.

The delegates discussed the Colonial Office's dispatch to Caribbean Governors advocating greater unity and co-operation, the ultimate goal of full self-government and the desire that demands for federation should come from within the region. Richard Hart spoke of the need to develop the British West Indies as a single economic unit so as to create stable and viable communities. It was Jamaica's retreat from this position fifteen years later that contributed to the demise of the Federation.

The Montego Bay Conference was held in September 1947, to discuss the closer association of the British West Indies. It was attended by 22 delegates from all the colonies, by representatives of the Colonial Development and Welfare Organization and by the British Representative to the Caribbean Commission. Bustamante, representing Jamaica, was cool about a "federation of paupers" which he saw as a way for the British government to prevent self-government and keep the colonies enchained. Without self-government he saw little point in federation. Norman Manley, representing the Caribbean Commission, spoke passionately in favour of federation, a position in line with most other representatives:

> It would be an irony the like of which history has never known, that a community with that ambition of nationhood, having been offered this chance of

amalgamation which is its only hope of a real political destiny, were to refuse that offer. Dare we refuse it and condemn ourselves and our generation for all time at the bar of history? I say that we dare not.

The Montego Bay Conference was the height of enthusiasm for closer association and West Indian unity. It was followed by a Standing Closer Association Committee to look at possible constitutions, forms of judiciary, customs and tariff problems and laws.

Although representing an important step closer towards federation, the Reports produced by this Committee threw up such sharp differences of opinion that the British Virgin Islands and British Guiana decided against joining a federation. British Honduras was also cautious of joining. The goodwill that had been generated at Montego Bay was in danger of evaporating in the light of the reality of what federation would entail. Yet despite reservations, all the other countries in the British West Indies decided to opt for federation. A wider Caribbean market would aid industrialization; freedom of movement would diffuse population pressures; a greater international status would be achieved, and sources of international capital be more readily tapped. What was probably the most persuasive argument in the discussion, however, was the shared feeling of anti-colonialism and the demand for self-government.

**19   Norman Manley, representing Jamaica, signs the report of the final meeting of the British Caribbean Federation Conference held in London in February 1956. The purpose of this conference was to make the final decisions before federation became a reality. It led to the passing of the British Caribbean Act in August 1956 to establish a federal union among the British Caribbean colonies.**

**20 Lord Hailes, first Governor-General of the short-lived Federation of the West Indies, takes the oath of office in Port-of-Spain, Trinidad.**

## THE FEDERATION OF THE WEST INDIES

Eleven years passed between the Montego Bay Conference and the establishment of the Federation, on 3 January 1958. These years were filled with political action designed both to lead to federation and, perhaps not intentionally, to cut the ground away from beneath it. Meetings took place in Britain and in the West Indies which led to the British Caribbean Act of 1956, establishing a federal union amongst the colonies taking part. Some of the most passionate discussion, however, had been spent on the site of the federal capital and Parliament. The 1950 "Rance" Report had recommended Trinidad, but some of the smaller islands objected on the grounds that this would further add to the influence of Trinidad, which was already the richest country. A three-man committee of non-West Indians was set up which suggested Barbados, Jamaica and Trinidad, in that order. Their suggestion was ignored and Trinidad was finally chosen with Chaguaramas as the site, one of the areas leased to the US in the 1940 "Destroyers Deal" with Britain. The US were asked to give up their base and although unwilling to do so, agreed to review the position of the base within a decade. Discussions over the ownership of the base, which Dr Williams made an act of principle, dragged on until 1970.

As federation came closer to becoming reality, it became sadly apparent that there was no longer any real enthusiasm for the idea in the West Indies. The real driving force for federation had been a small articulate group of politicians united in their opposition to colonialism. Many of them were now looking for self-government. Norman Manley, a consistent champion of the idea, was known to express his doubts for the venture, at the same time continuing to speak with great confidence about the future of federation. However, federation represented one step on the way to full independence.

From the outset it was obvious that this was not to be a strong federation. None of the governments involved was prepared to contribute more than the minimum to guarantee the administration of the organization. Jamaica was unwilling to lower its tariff and Trinidad was unwilling to allow unrestricted immigration from the other islands. There was no common coinage nor postage, no customs union and no freedom of movement between the islands.

The disparities of power and size seemed magnified within the Federation. Jamaica and Trinidad overshadowed every other country, accounting, as they did, for seven-eighths of the population and three-quarters of the wealth. Jamaica, the largest and second richest country to Trinidad, accounted for a little over half of the population of the West Indies. Had allotment of seats to the Federal Parliament been based on population, Jamaica could have ended up with a hundred and ten. As a compromise, Jamaica finally accepted seventeen of the forty-five seats.

There was little other evidence of a willingness to compromise and as federation approached, it was becoming clear that closer union would require sacrifice without too many advantages in return.

## THE FAILURE OF FEDERATION

The West Indies Federation was short-lived, collapsing in 1962. The enthusiasm of Montego Bay had all but gone by 1958, so its rapid decline and fall was, perhaps, inevitable. Why did the Federation fail? The British government was the immediate and obvious scapegoat. Certainly, after the Second World War, Britain no longer possessed the resources nor the desire to maintain an Empire on a pre-war scale and was looking to lose some of its colonial responsibilities. If that was so, then the British government's duty was far in excess of the miserly $2 million it donated to the Federation, a point made with some force by a Trinidadian representative to the UN in 1964:

> An administering power is not entitled to extract for centuries all that can be got out of a colony and when that has been done to relieve itself of the obligations by the conferment of a formal but meaningless – meaningless because it cannot possibly be supported – political independence. Justice requires that reparations be made to the country that has suffered the ravages of colonialism before that country is expected to face up to the problems and difficulties that will immediately beset it upon independence.

Britain's role in the failure of the Federation should not be minimized, nor should that of the West Indian leaders themselves. The political ambitions of politicians, together with personal antagonism, reduced the chances that federation could work. Differences rather than the spirit of unity were stressed. At Federal conferences there was little discussion nor room for manoeuvre, as individual West Indian leaders had already made their positions public. C.L.R. James, at the time Secretary to the West Indies Federal Labour Party, describes the leaders:

> devoid of programme and consideration for the people, they saw federation and met among themselves only to arrange what their governments would get and what they would lose. That is always an important part in any political discussion. But if you are discussing nothing else, the result is always

the violent quarrels, in fact the unseemly quarrels for that is what they were, by which these gentlemen broke up the Federation and disgraced the West Indian people. (*Party Politics in the West Indies*, Trinidad, 1962)

The two largest countries, Jamaica and Trinidad, have a special responsibility for the failure of federation. Jamaican attitudes at the time, as well as subsequently, epitomise the worst aspects of West Indian insularity. Norman Manley deliberately kept out of federal politics, and this resulted, inexorably, in the withdrawal of Jamaica from the Federation. The Jamaican referendum of 1961 was overwhelmingly in favour of secession, leading to the break-up of the Federation the next year. Jamaica's attitude showed the worst aspects of nationalism, at the expense of the other countries of the West Indies. Both Jamaica and Trinidad left the Federation because their size and power made it possible for them to achieve independence and development without the nuisance value of the smaller islands.

Trinidadians were not given the choice of a referendum, they were simply informed of their government's decision to withdraw from the Federation. This gave Dr Williams the opportunity to form a union between Trinidad and the Eastern Caribbean states that would adequately have reflected Trinidad's power and prestige in the area. He chose not to do so.

No sooner was the Federation dead, than the people of the West Indies showed their interest in other forms of regional co-operation.

## OTHER ATTEMPTS AT CO-OPERATION

Had the Federation of the West Indies had the same cohesion and dynamism as the West Indies Cricket Team, it would certainly not have foundered as it did. Nor was cricket the only workable form of co-operation in the West Indies. The University of the West Indies, which resulted from federation, has been maintained in the region with a growing reputation for excellence.

The Caribbean Development Bank (CDB) was set up in 1970 and the subsequent admission of Venezuela and Colombia bodes well for the future inclusion of other, non-English-speaking, members of the Caribbean. In addition to the CDB, a Caribbean Free Trade Area (CARIFTA) was established in 1966, which all the former members of the Federation joined, along with Guyana, Barbados and Antigua. In 1973, under the Treaty of Chaguaramas, CARIFTA was enlarged to form the Caribbean Community and Common Market (CARICOM).

The usefulness of CARICOM can be seen from Jamaica's record of trade with other Caribbean states, which increased more than six times in the first six years of its existence. Other countries have shown similar improvements in trade. CARICOM is not just about trade, however, but about political integration, and here the organization has been less successful. Meetings have been held under CARICOM's umbrella that have brought West Indian leaders together, but the aim of political and economic co-operation still remains an ideal.

The difficulties of even holding a summit meeting of West Indian leaders in the early 1980s was apparent when both the site and date of the meeting had to be frequently changed so as to enable all the heads of government to get together at one time. The meeting was finally held at Ocho Rios in Jamaica in November 1982, the previous summit having been held seven years before in St Kitts. Except for a special meeting in Trinidad in 1976, to discuss the University of the West Indies, plans for other summits had come to nothing. CARICOM has, therefore, limped along, holding meetings at low levels, the organization exhibiting all the nationalism and pettiness that characterized the earlier Federation.

Economic pressures brought the heads of government together again after the Ocho Rios meeting, which had been held mainly for the discussion of political issues. Despite bickering between some of the states, the meeting was considered a success because it brought all the member states together and added Bahamas to its ranks (though deciding against the inclusion of the Dominican Republic). The disunity and lack of a regional approach to issues, however, was all too reminiscent of the Federation.

The invasion of Grenada by United States armed forces in October 1983 led to further tension within CARICOM. Jamaica and Barbados, along with Eastern Caribbean countries, supported the

21 The sharing of expertise on fishing is just one example of collaboration between Cuba and her neighbours in the Caribbean.

invasion, whilst Trinidad and Guyana and the other CARICOM members strongly opposed it. Their opposition was based upon the need to ensure the right of Caribbean countries to determine their own destinies. With the stronger presence and influence of the United States in the Caribbean, both Guyana and Trinidad expected to be "punished", economically or diplomatically, by the United States for their opposition. In November 1983 Trinidad was placed "on alert" in the expectation of destabilization by the US.

In addition to CARICOM, the Caribbean states have set up a number of organizations, mainly of an economic nature. Most of the Caribbean states are agricultural-based economies and the forms of organization set up tend to reflect this fact.

*The Committee for Caribbean Development and Co-operation (CDCC)* was set up in Havana in 1975, to bring about different ways of economic co-operation in the region. The aim is more rapid economic development.

*The Multinational Caribbean Fleet (NAMUCAR)* was founded in San Jose, Costa Rica, in 1975, to develop maritime transport for the benefit of the region so as to counter the domination by, predominantly, North American vessels which, in 1975, accounted for 88% of traffic.

*The Eastern Caribbean Common Market (ECCM)* was formed in Grenada in 1968, designed to eliminate customs duties, tariffs and restrictions to trade between member countries, to facilitate the movement of productive resources and to consolidate existing economic relations. The Eastern Caribbean states have benefited little from CARICOM because of their small size and limited industrialization; their own common market emerged out of their own particular problems of economic and social development.

*The Central American Common Market (MCCA)* was formed in Managua, Nicaragua, in 1960, to bring about free trade in the area. Members are drawn from Central American countries bordering the Caribbean.

*The Latin American Economic System (SELA),* formed in Panama in 1975, whilst primarily composed of mainland Latin American countries, is, nonetheless, involved in the Caribbean and has given support to Caribbean organizations like NAMUCAR and COMUNBANA, the organization of banana producers.

Other organizations which emerged in the 1970s to protect and develop primary products include *The Group of Latin American and Caribbean Sugar Producers (GEPLACEA)* which was formed in Mexico in 1974 as a consultative body to protect the interests of sugar producers in the region; *The Union of Banana Exporting Countries (UPEB),* founded in Panama in 1974; and *The Intergovernmental Association of Bauxite Producers* which is of particular interest to Jamaica, Guyana, and Suriname. Jamaica is the second largest producer of bauxite in the world and the largest exporter; Suriname and Guyana are the third and fourth largest producers. Between them, the three countries account for two-thirds of the world total production of bauxite.

Trinidad-Tobago, Curacao, Venezuela and Mexico belong to the *Organization of Oil Exporting Countries (OPEC).*

Members of the former British, French and Dutch colonies have special rights in the *European Economic Community (EEC),* through the Lomé Convention of 1976.

Cuba is a member of the *Council of Mutual Economic Assistance (CAME or COMECON),* which is a common market between the socialist countries.

---

## YOUNG HISTORIAN

A
1 List all the factors, in order of importance, that have hindered co-operation in the Caribbean.
2 Find out more about the rights of Caribbean countries, if any, in the EEC.
3 How has Cuba been able to help other Caribbean countries?
4 What have been the main difficulties for CARICOM?
5 Find out more about any *two* Caribbean organizations.

B
1 You are a Cuban doctor working in Jamaica in the 1970s. Describe a typical day.
2 As a journalist, what questions would you have asked Dr Eric Williams about Trinidad's withdrawal from the Federation of the West Indies?

C
Compose headlines for (a) the US "Destroyers Deal" with Britain, (b) Federation Day in the British Caribbean, (c) the failure of Federation.

D
Using different colours for each organization, indicate membership of each Caribbean organization on a map of the region.

# INDEPENDENCE

After the Second World War Britain had neither the resources nor the desire to maintain an Empire along pre-war lines. In the Caribbean the United States was, anyway, poised and prepared to assume the role of "policeman" for the area and little pressure was required to make Britain divest itself of this piece of Empire.

Haiti became independent in 1804; Puerto Rico tried, in 1868, to declare its independence from Spain with its "Grito de Lares", but was ceded to the United States at the Treaty of Paris that ended

**22 The Trinidad Carnival in 1953, Coronation Year, was both topical and demonstrated the British connection – which was to continue even after independence.**

the Spanish-Cuban-American War in 1898. Cuba gained its independence, in name only, in that same year, after a long and bloody battle against Spain throughout the nineteenth century; but it became a virtual colony of the United States.

The establishment of the Federation of the West Indies had, in that area of the Caribbean, begun a process of political discussion and awareness, bringing to the surface demands that could only be met through full independence. Jamaica and Trinidad-Tobago, the largest and richest of the islands, gained theirs in 1962, St Kitts-Nevis had to wait until 1983, so that just five tiny islands remain still in a modified colonial position. The French colonies of Martinique, Guadeloupe and

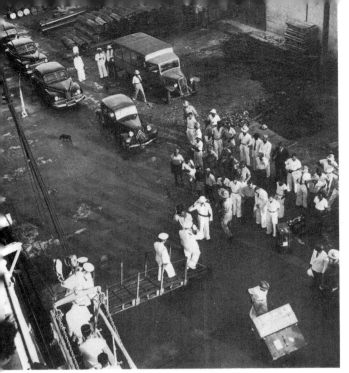

**23** Citroen cars and trucks form part of the welcoming committee at Point-A-Pitre, Guadeloupe for the arriving French Prefect. Guadeloupe, and the rest of the former French colonies, are now regarded as separate Departments within metropolitan France.

the tiny islands in their charge, along with French Guyana, remain (in 1984) overseas Departments of France with representation in the French Senate and in the National Assembly.

The Dutch Caribbean islands of Aruba and Curacao, along with Suriname, were made equal in status to Holland in 1954; Suriname was given its independence in 1975.

Haiti had suffered continuous economic and political turmoil throughout the nineteenth century. In the period 1804 to 1879, for example,

**24** "Baby Doc" Duvalier, who succeeded his father "Papa Doc" Duvalier in Haiti in 1971, surrounded by armed militia and the infamous Tonton Macoutes, his private army.

Haiti saw out about seventy presidents who did little to ensure the country's security and growth, but rather enhanced their own positions. The twentieth century began in economic and social crisis. President after President borrowed money abroad, using Haiti's customs receipts as security. By 1915 the country was bankrupt. The United States, concerned about the island's proximity to the Panama Canal and the involvement of France and Germany in the country's affairs, decided upon intervention and military occupation. In 1914 more than two thousand US Marines landed and occupied the country, in the process removing half a million dollars worth of gold from the National Bank, for "safe-keeping" in New York. The occupation, which lasted to 1934, left no mark of a positive nature on Haiti. Political unrest began as soon as the occupying forces left, and went on until 1957, when François Duvalier – Papa Doc – was elected to power, ushering in a period in Haiti's history of unprecedented ruthlessness and brutality.

Papa Doc kept in power through the use of his own private army, the Tonton Macoutes, and by replacing all government administrators by his own appointees; through the use of *Vodun* – Voodoo – he struck terror into all spheres of Haitian society. Needless to say, his period of office (he died in 1971) was marked by a decline in all areas of economic or social activity. Poverty, malnutrition, disease and ignorance are the enduring monument to Papa Doc.

Jean Claude Duvalier, who succeeded his father in 1971, had made little improvement to Haiti's sorry lot by the 1980s.

---

## CUBA

---

Cubans say that their struggle for independence began in the nineteenth century, with the conspiracies of the 1820s and '30s, the Ten Years War against Spain from 1868 to 1878, the Little War that followed it, when Antonio Maceo refused to stop fighting, short of full independence, through the full-scale war of liberation against Spain from 1895-98, organized and led by the legendary José Martí, and through various forms of struggle on into the twentieth century, until finally successful in 1959.

Cuba was virtually an American colony until the early 1960s. American interests controlled most, and certainly the most important parts, of Cuba's economy; 75% of all arable land, 90% of services, 40% of the sugar industry, were all in foreign (mostly US) hands. Most of Cuba's wealth came from sugar, which had produced a stagnant, lopsided, inequitable society by the 1950s. Intolerable disparities existed between town and country, the latter resembling another land because of its poverty and backwardness. Housing, health provision, education, sanitation – if they existed at all – were not found in the country areas.

Such inequalities and divisions in society aroused demands for change which were never far below the surface. Batista, Cuba's "strongman" since the 1930s, exacerbated tensions by taking power in a coup in 1952. The following year, on 26 July 1953, Fidel Castro launched an attack on the Moncada army barracks in Santiago de Cuba, Cuba's second city, beginning the struggle for liberation all over again. The purpose of this attack was simple and direct; to overthrow the dictator Batista and to replace him with a government committed to reform.

It was not to be. The attack on the Moncada ended in failure and disaster, with many of the "Moncadistas" captured, tortured, then executed by Batista's police. Fidel Castro was himself caught and put into prison on the Isle of Pines. Released in 1956, as a result of popular pressure for an amnesty, he organized his forces – now called the 26th July Movement, after the attack on the Moncada. Returning to Cuba after exile in Mexico, despite heavy losses of men and equipment on landing, Fidel Castro regrouped and then enlarged his forces to take control of Cuba two years later, causing Batista to flee the country, militarily and politically defeated.

Castro's revolutionary government replaced that of Batista's corrupt and inept regime and immediately set itself the task of redressing the imbalances and inequalities of the past and so realizing the nationalistic ambitions of the earlier struggles for independence. The Cuban Revolution, which has had more than its share of false starts and failures, has been able to break away from its repressive and negative relationship with the United States and begin a

**25** Dr Eric Williams, Trinidad and Tobago's Prime Minister (in dark glasses), at his country's Independence Conference in London in 1962.

**26** The tiny island of Anguilla "seceded" from St Kitts and Nevis in 1969 to be occupied by troops and British "Bobbies" sent to restore Britain's authority.

process of struggle against backwardness and underdevelopment. The achievements of the Cuban Revolution in health, education, housing, employment and welfare provision have made Cuba a model for development in the Caribbean, since it has dealt definitively with the problems which still plague the rest of the area.

## THE DOMINICAN REPUBLIC

Dominican history has many superficial similarities with that of Cuba and Haiti in the twentieth century. The century began in economic and political chaos, under the watchful eye of the United States, which, in 1905, took over responsibility for the country's customs and foreign debts. Full military occupation lasted from 1916 to 1924. The unrest which followed was only put down by the dictatorial hand of Trujillo, Dominica's President from 1930 to his assassination in 1961. Throughout that time Trujillo, as we have seen, was wholeheartedly supported by the United States which again

**27** The 1963-64 crisis in Guyana involved fighting and rioting between East Indians and people of African origin as well as accusations against Cheddi Jagan of "communism". Trade unions played a large part in the unrest of the period.

invaded the country in 1965 to keep Juan Bosch, a socialist, from the presidency. Since that time the Dominican Republic has enjoyed relative stability under the presidency of Balaguer and Jorge Blanco and a close political and economic relationship with the United States.

---

## THE "BRITISH CARIBBEAN"

---

Most of the former British colonies in the Caribbean became independent in the twentieth century; by the start of the 1980s only five had failed to do so and that was because of their small size. Their independence came from the marked political awakening of the 1940s and '50s and, in the cases of Jamaica and Trinidad, from the levels of economic development attained. Federation was but a step on the way to full political independence, the pursuit of which was one of the reasons for the collapse of the organization.

Jamaica and Trinidad both decided, separately, to seek independence outside the Federation, their decisions reinforced by the impending entry of Britain to the European Economic Community (EEC), which they saw as a threat to West Indian exports of sugar and bananas. Further suspicion and resentment were caused by the 1961 Commonwealth Immigration Act, the first of a number of such pieces of legislation, that closed off the safety valve to West Indian population growth.

With Jamaica and Trinidad making their own ways in the region, largely, it should be said, because of the personal idiosyncrasies of their leaders, it was left to the other, smaller islands to make their own way as best they could, either in a federation among themselves or with Trinidad taking a responsible lead. Trinidad was not prepared to take on such a responsibility and so negotiations involving Barbados and the others were abandoned in 1965.

Jamaica under Bustamante's leadership and Dr Williams' Trinidad became sovereign states in 1962. Barbados, the most developed of the other islands, became independent in 1966. In the same year it was agreed that Antigua with Barbuda and Redonda, tiny islands close by, St Kitts, Nevis-Anguilla, Dominica, Grenada, St Lucia and St Vincent should become Associated States with Great Britain – that is, self-governing in internal matters but with Britain taking on responsibility for defence and foreign affairs. British Honduras became independent Belize in 1964.

British Guiana's steps towards independence have been the most fraught of any of the former British colonies. In 1953 the first elections under conditions of universal adult suffrage were held. The People's Progressive Party (PPP) won eighteen of the twenty-four seats of the elected legislature. Government was still of the Crown Colony type made up, predominantly, of officials nominated by the Colonial Office. The PPP was a Marxist party and its election was clearly unpalatable to Whitehall. Within 133 days the Colonial Office intervened, dissolved the government and suspended the Constitution that had given Guiana a degree of internal self-government.

The People's Progressive Party's success had been based on its ability to unite the African, black, and the East Indian, brown, sections of Guianese society. This unity was lost in 1955 when the party split, one faction continuing as the PPP, led by Cheddi Jagan, the other led by Forbes Burnham, Jagan's former deputy in the PPP. This became the People's National Congress (PNC) in 1957. When elections were held in 1957 and in 1961, Cheddi Jagan's party won both times, but a left-wing government was considered unacceptable to both British and American interests in the region. A manoeuvre, involving Britain and America, with a special role being played by the United States' Central Intelligence Agency (CIA), provoked internal unrest that led to Jagan's persecution and imprisonment. British Guiana became independent Guyana in 1962. Forbes Burnham was installed in office after the

1964 elections and has remained in power ever since, by increasingly repressive means.

Independence is a beginning, not an end, for Caribbean countries. It incurs taking on awesome responsibilities for the management of the country's affairs, after centuries of mismanagement with little or no interest in the Caribbean or its people. Attitudes and structures shaped in the past continue to assert themselves to the present day. Recent experiences have shown the problem of trying to dislodge this legacy of the past.

## YOUNG HISTORIAN

**A**

1 Make a chronological list of dates of Independence in the different Caribbean countries.
2 Were Caribbean "suspicions" of Britain in the early 1960s justified?
3 Find out more about Britain's, and the US's, role in Guyana in the early 1960s.
4 Write brief biographies of José Martí and Antonio Maceo.
5 How have successive British Immigration Acts affected the Caribbean?
6 Why did the United States invade the Dominican Republic in 1965; Grenada in 1983? Are there connections between the two invasions?

**B**

1 You are in Haiti and have the opportunity to interview "Baby Doc" Duvalier. What ten questions would you ask?
2 As a Representative of one of the French Caribbean islands, what demands would you make in the French Senate?

**C**

Compose headlines for (a) the Spanish defeat in Cuba in 1898, (b) the death of "Papa Doc" in 1971, (c) the assassination of Trujillo in 1961, and (d) Independence day in either Jamaica or Trinidad.

**D**

Design *either* a sculpture *or* a poster *or* a set of stamps to celebrate Independence day in any one Caribbean country.

# PERSISTENT PROBLEMS

The dramatic changes that have occurred in the Caribbean in the twentieth century — independence for the bulk of the former British colonies; a socialist revolution in Cuba posing a challenge to the region; closer involvement of the United States in the region — have not eliminated the diverse economic, social and political problems which oppressed most of the countries as they entered the century. Haiti, for example, has progressed little in this century; Cuba, on the other hand, has shown dramatic improvements in the first twenty-five years of its revolution, yet is still confronting problems. Economic problems abound, not least because of the historical legacy of the region being developed as a source of cheap agricultural products for distant, more developed, markets.

Cuba, insulated from some of the economic problems of its Caribbean neighbours because of its membership of COMECON and long-term guaranteed prices for its products, nonetheless was forced, along with other Third World countries, to apply to Western European Banks in the early 1980s for a rescheduling of its debts.

## SUGAR

Sugar, in the 1980s, is still of as central importance to the wealth and prosperity (usually otherwise) of Caribbean economies as it has been since the eighteenth century. A rise or fall of just one cent per pound on the World Sugar Market can spell prosperity or depression to Caribbean sugar producers and the people who depend upon it for their livelihood. Both during and immediately after the First World War the price of sugar was high on the World Market, though falling to disastrously low levels after 1929 and the onset of the world depression. Lord Olivier, in his survey of British West Indian sugar production in 1930, pointed to the need for greater assistance in the form of preferential protection (higher prices and purchases of Caribbean rather than European beet sugar), but this was not forthcoming from Britain, nor from other countries, until 1934 when the West Indian sugar industry, and the people who depended upon it, were suffering the most acute distress. The depression of the 1930s in the developed world was a social and economic catastrophe for the underdeveloped world. In the Caribbean the period was one of extreme hardship for the mass of the people. The ups and downs of the sugar industry illustrate how the Caribbean economies are at the mercy of external forces.

Sugar production increased throughout the Caribbean in the late 1930s, under the protection of Imperial Preference in the British colonies and because of the American sugar quota system in Cuba, Puerto Rico and the US Virgin Islands. The International Sugar Regulation of 1937 was an attempt to increase prices through the control of production on the basis of quotas. The political unrest throughout the area from the mid- to late 1930s had been, in part, an expression of the distress experienced in the sugar industry.

The Second World War, like the First, brought a stimulus to the Caribbean economies in general, and to sugar in particular. The price rose in response to growing world demand for cane sugar, as beet sugar areas in Europe had been decimated in the war. Sugar production in the British West Indies was controlled after the war by the Commonwealth Sugar Agreement of 1951, and in all sugar-producing countries by the International Sugar Agreement, from 1953. The agreement lasted until 1960 and the degree of protection it offered was sufficient to save the sugar industry from collapse.

Beet sugar production got under way again in Europe immediately after the war and its growth within the area of the EEC has been *the* major problem for Caribbean sugar producers in the 1970s and '80s. Indeed, when the International Sugar Organization (ISO) was meeting in Geneva in 1983 to work out a new International Sugar Agreement (ISA), the system having broken down, observers were of the opinion that it was "all up to the EEC". Production by European countries, especially France and Britain, of beet sugar heavily subsidized by European consumers and using highly efficient, capital-intensive farming methods, has resulted in a sugar "mountain" alongside those of butter and beef in the midst, no doubt, of the EEC's "wine lake". This production of subsidized agricultural products, within the EEC, which no member country apparently wants, has been catastrophic for Caribbean sugar producers.

**28  Open-cast mining, Kingston, Jamaica. Bauxite has been a mixed blessing for Jamaica and Guyana. It has provided employment, as an alternative to agriculture, but has led to a considerable degree of control of the economy residing outside the country.**

Prices, which stood at 66 cents per pound in the mid-1970s fell to single figures, 6, 7 and 8 cents per pound, thereafter to the 1980s.

---

## MINERALS

---

The Caribbean is not rich in minerals but there are considerable reserves of bauxite, from which aluminium is made, in Jamaica, Guyana and Suriname; Trinidad possesses both oil and asphalt; Cuba has the third largest nickel resources in the world, as well as amounts of cobalt, manganese and other metals.

Oil production began in Trinidad in 1909-10, expanding dramatically under the pressures of the First and Second World Wars. Oil in Trinidad has given that country the resources upon which economic growth could begin. The industry provides employment for some twenty thousand Trinidadians and has spawned numerous chemical and other industries based on petroleum by-products. Oil and related products account for some 80% of Trinidad's exports which until the late 1970s provided Trinidad with a healthy surplus on its balance of payments. However, along with other oil-producing countries, Trinidad's revenue has been falling off because of a drop in demand for oil. By the 1980s this was resulting in a downturn in the country's economic growth.

The discovery of bauxite in the 1940s gave Jamaica a much-needed alternative to agriculture, which dominated the economy to 1950. It was discovered that Jamaica is covered almost entirely in a layer of bauxite actually richer than that of Guyana. In both countries, bauxite development has been dominated by North American companies. In 1977, for example, Jamaica and Guyana provided the US with 65% of its bauxite. Haiti, Suriname and the Dominican Republic supplied a further 25%.

The Caribbean area is a major source of bauxite, yet studies have shown that the benefits derived from it are accrued elsewhere. The greatest profit from bauxite lies in its smelting and conversion into aluminium products. Most of this process occurs in the United States and Canada. Plants for smelting exist in Jamaica, Guyana and Suriname, but most ores are exported for treatment in North

**29  Oil refinery, Kingston, Jamaica. Since 1973, when the OPEC countries raised oil prices, Caribbean sources of oil and oil refining have become of strategic importance to the United States.**

America. Hence the Caribbean has benefited little from this natural resource. Guyana's economy actually stagnated in the period 1940-60, despite the existence of bauxite which made Alcan, which mines Guyanese bauxite, the world's second largest aluminium company.

In Jamaica, the production of bauxite has led to land shortages for agriculture, as bauxite companies bought up 100,000 acres of land to control the ore extraction which is 100% controlled by American companies. In 1974 the government of Michael Manley in Jamaica tried to raise the amount they received from the aluminium

companies. The result was that the companies simply cut back on their production of bauxite and alumina from Jamaica and doubled production in Guinea. Manley also found it difficult to raise international loans as a result of his "meddling" with the bauxite industry. In Guyana, Forbes Burnham was no more fortunate than Manley in trying to wrest control and greater revenues for his country from the bauxite companies. Nationalizations began in 1971, but Guyana soon discovered the strengths of the multi-national aluminium companies who were determined to extract the best compensation possible. This was in the knowledge that Guyana's mineral resources had been depleted of the most easily extracted bauxite, and that Guinea and Australia were the preferred suppliers. Even nationalized, the Guyanese bauxite still has to be sold to the multinational companies.

Cuba *was* able to wrest control of its resources after 1959, but this has not always had immediately positive results. After the difficulties in the early 1960s of simply keeping the industry going without US technology and expertise, the Cuban nickel industry has suffered from a US embargo that keeps it out of US, and any other, markets the US government can pressure. French stainless steel, which contains Cuban nickel, was only allowed into the US after an "assurance" from France's President, Mr Mitterand, that, in fact, it did not. Most Cuban nickel and other minerals go to the Soviet Union and other COMECON countries. Cuba and the Soviet Union are beginning to make their presence felt in the international metals market through their production of nickel. In the Cuban Five Year Plan,

**30  Loading pitch from Trinidad's pitch lake, a vast natural resource.**

which began in 1981, nickel has been allotted a crucial role as a major contributor to economic growth to the year 2000.

## TOURISM

The Caribbean islands offer a tropical climate and breathtakingly beautiful scenery and beaches; tourism, since the 1960s, has become an important sector of the Caribbean economy. Tourism to Jamaica doubled between 1964 and 1974, largely because of the closing-off of Cuba as a tourist centre. However, despite the obvious – and increasing – importance of tourism to the Caribbean, it is questionable to what extent the region benefits from it. For some countries tourism has become what sugar was, or in some cases still is – an economic sector around which every other activity depends. A bad season can have devastating consequences.

Even socialist Cuba, from the 1970s, has depended increasingly on tourism for its hard currency earnings. Over 100 thousand tourists from Canada alone visited Cuba during the winter months of the early 1980s – a fact not lost on the other islands competing with Cuba for the tourist trade. Cuba has tried, however, to minimize the social damage that tourism can cause. Firstly, Cuba has attempted to ensure that the minimum of imports are sucked in by tourist demand; foodstuffs, for example, enjoyed by tourists to Cuba are almost entirely produced in the country itself. This contrasts markedly with other Caribbean countries, more closely connected with North America, where the bulk of foodstuffs, even including tropical fruits that could easily be grown locally, are air-freighted in. Cuba has also tried to minimize the effects of tourism on its own population by making tourist facilities available to its own people as well as to those from abroad. Again this contrasts with the rest of the area where the locals' usual contact with tourist facilities is through work, which causes resentment and, sometimes, racial friction – for the typical tourist to the Caribbean is a white, middle-class, usually American, person who spends his or her time in a tourist enclave that carefully shields him or her from the often squalid reality of daily Caribbean life. The racial tensions that exist in other Caribbean countries are no longer present in Cuba which has got rid of them, along with the begging and prostitution that go hand-in-hand with tourism elsewhere in the region.

## SOCIAL FACTORS

The fragmentation of the Caribbean continues to hold back the unification of the region as well as attempts at economic and political cooperation. The stresses within CARICOM in the wake of the invasion of Grenada in 1983 showed all too clearly the fragility of the sense of Caribbean unity.

As we have seen, the reasons for the "Balkanization" of the Caribbean have their roots in its geography, and in a history which has introduced a variety of racial and cultural elements with profound consequences for the present. In only one country, Cuba, have the different racial and cultural strands been combined in the "melting pot", to form a cohesive society apparently free from racial tensions. In most other countries, the links with the old, or new, metropolitan countries, be they Britain, Holland, France, the United States or Canada, have resulted in the stratification of society along racial lines. In Puerto Rico, one of the more "integrated" societies in the Caribbean, the black person has little chance of rising economically, socially or intellectually. Barbados is infamous for the extent of the stratification of its society along lines of colour, with subtle degrees of colour determining one's position in society. It is partly for this reason that Barbados is known as "Little England" by its Caribbean neighbours.

The explosive mixture of East Indian and African still ticks away in Trinidad, Guyana and Suriname. In Trinidad, where the East Indian population is the fastest growing one, young, dynamic Indian intellectuals are challenging the traditional African dominance. First it was in the civil service and the professions, later in the political arena. How soon before the first East Indian Prime Minister in Trinidad?

In Guyana recent political developments have been along ethnic lines. A clear division between the East Indian and African populations resulted in racial massacres between 1962 and 1964.

Forbes Burnham is only able to continue to represent the black minority in Guyana (about 30% of the population) through totalitarian and repressive means. Although Burnham has received Indian support at election time, the racial problem in Guyana is a pressing one.

A white bias affects most other Caribbean countries. Even in Cuba, which is experiencing a socialist revolution, ideas of the cultural and technological superiority of the United States, for example, are a part of the folk-mythology, which played no small part in the "exodus" from Mariel in 1981. Nowhere is this bias more evident than in the cultural penetration that has accompanied the economic penetration of the region. A barrage of foreign, largely US, movies, television and radio programmes emphasize the advantages of an alien way of life. Flows of tourists provide the living proof, if proof were needed, of the superiority of the US/Canadian/British way. In his visit to Trinidad, V.S. Naipaul in *The Middle Passage* comments:

> To be modern is to ignore local products and to use those advertised in American magazines. The excellent coffee which is grown in Trinidad is used only by the poor and a few middle-class English expatriates. Everyone else drinks Nescafe or Maxwell House or Chase and Sanborn, which is more expensive but is advertised in the magazines and therefore acceptable. The elegant and comfortable Morris chairs, made from local wood by local craftsmen, are not modern and have disappeared except from the houses of the poor. Imported tubular steel furniture, plastic straw chairs from Hong Kong and spindly cast-iron chairs have taken their place.

Despite this influence, perhaps because of it, Caribbean people, especially those who have had little or no contact with colonial society, are looking not only for greater economic self-control but also for their own national and cultural identity. The Rastafarians of Jamaica and elsewhere are one of the more obvious expressions of rebellion against the materialism and consumerism that have been developed in the modern Caribbean. Less obvious, but no less important, are the wearing of Afro-hair styles and African styles of dress, or the more informal kinds of dress like the Cariba jacket made famous by Michael Manley of Jamaica. CARIFESTA, the pan-Caribbean arts festival, first held in Guyana in 1972, has become the meeting point for dance, music, theatre, poetry and the plastic arts,

throughout the entire Caribbean. It is the regular proof of the cultural explosion that has occurred in the Caribbean from the 1960s. Caribbean artists and writers have gained confidence in the post-colonial environment that has enabled them to break out of the fetters imposed by the old colonial society. Their work shows the liberating effects of de-colonization.

## YOUNG HISTORIAN

**A**

1 Find out more about the state of Health and Education provision in the Caribbean. Make a "league table" of rates of illiteracy, infant mortality rates, and life expectancy in the Caribbean.
2 Why haven't Caribbean countries stopped producing sugar?
3 Has tourism benefited the Caribbean?
4 Are Caribbean countries entirely dependent on more developed countries?
5 In what ways, and with what success, have Caribbean countries tried to protect their natural resources?

**B**

How would you deal with the social and economic problems existing in the Caribbean in the 1980s?

**C**

1 Design a poster for CARIFESTA.
2 On a map of the Caribbean, mark the range of economic activities.

**31  Rastafarians in Jamaica oppose the materialism of Western society.**

# MIGRATION: THE SAFETY VALVE?

## POPULATION TRENDS

The population of the Caribbean has grown throughout the twentieth century, as a result of improvements in medical care (especially its effect on infant mortality rates) and the eradication of diseases like malaria and yellow fever. Nowhere has this been more dramatically shown than in Cuba where, in the first twenty-five years of the revolution, health care has been developed to put Cubans on a par with North America and Western Europe. No longer do Cubans die of deficiency or epidemic diseases; now they suffer from stress, and may die of cancer or heart attacks. The number of doctors and nurses per head of the population is greater in Cuba than in most European countries; life expectancy is the same as in North America.

The record is much less spectacular in other Caribbean islands but, nonetheless, health conditions have improved dramatically, with implications for population growth. In Jamaica, for example, between 1921 and 1925 the infant mortality rate was 23.5 per thousand; by 1941-45 it had fallen to 12.9 per thousand. As traditional values, with regard to families and family size, remain unchanged, the result was a population increase that has continued to the present. Without emigration the effects of this rise in population would have been socially damaging. As it was, in the period 1946-60 the equivalent of one fifth of the natural increase in population emigrated. Hence, the net rate of emigration in the Caribbean is a more important statistic than natural increase.

## INTERNAL MIGRATION

It could be said that the Caribs were the first Caribbean internal migrants, long before the European invasion of the region. More recently migration has provided a safety valve to reduce social and economic pressures in times of crisis.

French planters from Haiti fled to Eastern Cuba with their families and slaves, to escape the slave revolt there at the start of the nineteenth century. Jamaica's labourers in their thousands contributed to the building of the Panama Canal and the establishment of the banana industry in Central America. Many Jamaicans and Barbadians settled in Cuba after short stints there as migrant workers during boom years. British Virgin Islanders have traditionally migrated to the more prosperous US Virgin Islands, in search of better work and living conditions.

## MIGRATION TO THE UNITED STATES

Migrants from the Caribbean as a whole went to the United States in the period 1910 to 1920, but this was curtailed by the Quota Acts of 1921 and 1924. The US has traditionally been a magnet to migrants from all over the world. In the 1950s a quarter of a million Puerto Ricans emigrated to the US; by the 1960s a third of Puerto Ricans lived on the mainland United States. Between 1962 and 1976 nearly a quarter of a million Jamaicans, Trinidadians, Guyanese and Barbadians were

32  Cubans leave the port of Camarioca in 1965 to
establish new lives in Miami in the United States.
Those who left Cuba at this time bitterly resented the
arrival of those from Mariel in 1981.

33  Many thousands of Haitian refugees have sought
asylum in the US, fleeing the cruel regime of father and
son, "Papa" and "Baby" Doc Duvalier.

allowed into the United States as emigrants. These more recent emigrants have consisted largely of skilled and semi-skilled workers and are said by some to represent a drain of skilled manpower from the Caribbean. They included some 8,000 medical personnel, doctors and nurses, whose departure added to the shortages of skilled workers in their own countries. Others have been unskilled workers, desperate to find work. Ten to fifteen thousand workers a year, mostly from Jamaica, travel to the US to work in agriculture for short periods of time, from one to nine months. Most are employed in the Florida cane fields, alongside Puerto Ricans and Mexicans similarly desperate for work. Conditions of work are often intolerable, yet neither they nor their governments have the power to bargain for better ones.

Emigration from Cuba to the United States has been one of the most highly publicized movements of people in the area. Many thousands of middle-class families fled in the early years of the Cuban revolution, fearful of its socialist ideology, taking with them into exile their opposition to the regime as well as their skills. In 1965 and 1968 airlifts arranged with the US government took away thousands more unsympathetic to the regime. Their departure was in sharp contrast to the exodus from Mariel, a port near Havana, in 1981, when 125,000 took the opportunity to leave on being told that anyone who wished to could leave the country. Whereas the first wave of exiles to the US were predominantly white, middle-class, skilled workers, the "Marielitos" were largely unskilled, with a high proportion of black people. Among their numbers, too, were criminal elements who had been given the choice of remaining in prison or going to the US. Most chose the latter course. Further immigration was halted by the US government in 1981 until the Cuban government is prepared to negotiate the repatriation of criminals too dangerous to be allowed on to American streets.

**34  6 September 1958. Norman Manley, Jamaica's Prime Minister at the time of the 1950s race riots, visits Notting Hill in London, the scene of some of the most unpleasant incidents.**

**35   10 September 1958. Norman Manley points to a poster common in Jamaica in the 1950s, which drew the attention of would-be emigrants to some of the drawbacks.**

**36   Their parents may have come from the Caribbean but this generation of young people's roots are in Britain.**

## EMIGRATION TO BRITAIN

West Indian emigration to Britain resulted from a desire to escape from poverty and unemployment and find in Britain the opportunities for advancement that were lacking at home. Contact with British culture through the centuries of colonial rule had prepared West Indians for their encounter with Britain, though for many it was to prove an unhappy experience.

The 1950s saw emigration to Britain on a huge scale, aided by cheap air and sea passages. British employers set up recruiting offices in the Caribbean. From 2,000 in 1953, immigration rose to 50,000 in 1960. By 1965 there were over 150,000 West Indian workers in Britain. They were a tiny proportion of the total number of immigrant workers in the country, but conspicuous because of their colour and flamboyant nature. Bitterness and resentment were caused in the British Caribbean, as well as among those West Indians already in Britain, by the decision of the British government in 1961 to introduce the Commonwealth Immigration Act that began the end to unrestricted entry into Britain, reducing the flow to insignificance by the 1980s. Caribbean immigrants to Britain made, as they continue to make, a positive contribution not only to the economy but also to the cultural richness and diversity of British society.

## EMIGRATION TO CANADA

Small numbers of people have emigrated from the Caribbean to settle in Canada, throughout the twentieth century. This was a natural outcome of the growth of trade between Canada and the Caribbean. The numbers of those emigrating to Canada were reduced after 1962, by the Canadian government's requirement that all immigrants should have reached a standard of education and training as to make them self-sufficient. In 1975 just over 4,500 West Indians emigrated to Canada; in 1976 the figure had fallen to just over 3,250.

## EMIGRATION FROM THE FRENCH AND DUTCH CARIBBEAN

The French Caribbean countries are plagued by the same social and economic ills as the rest of the region. A 1970 survey in Guadeloupe showed that only one person in three escaped total or partial unemployment. In Martinique, surveys in 1971 and 1972 showed that 60% of the working population were affected by unemployment or underemployment. The policy of the French government from the 1960s onwards has been to encourage emigration to France and this has been occurring in a continuous stream, but without causing any improvement in employment or living conditions. It is publicly recognized in the French Caribbean that the only way to advance is by leaving for France. Administrative positions are usually filled, at the same time, by a flow of functionaries from France.

The former Dutch colonies share the common social and economic problems of the region, not least unemployment. Large numbers of people from the old Dutch colonies have migrated to Holland. Almost half the population of Suriname went to Holland on the eve of its independence.

## YOUNG HISTORIAN

A
1  List the population of the major Caribbean countries for 1900, 1920, 1940, 1960 and 1980.
2  Find out more about the contribution of Caribbean people in (a) Britain, (b) the USA, and (c) Canada.
3  What were the main reasons for emigration to Britain from the Caribbean in the 1950s?

B
You are a Caribbean emigrant arriving in (a) London, (b) New York, and (c) Toronto. Write a letter home to your neighbours describing your experiences.

C
Write headlines for (a) the completion of the Panama Canal, stressing the contribution made by Caribbean migrant workers, (b) the arrival of the first Caribbean immigrants to Britain in the 1950s, and (c) the exodus from Mariel in Cuba in 1981.

D
Plot on a map the directions of migrants to and from the Caribbean.

# UNCLE SAM'S BACKYARD

The growth of American interest and involvement in the Caribbean has been one of the most obvious, if not *the* most obvious, developments in the area in the twentieth century. It could be said that US sights were trained on the Caribbean area for a century before but that it was only at the end of the nineteenth century that the US had the resources, as well as the political confidence, to take the region on. As the twentieth century reaches its end, there is not an area of the Caribbean that is untouched or unaffected by the power of the United States.

**37 Broad Street, Barbados, in 1927 already shows much evidence of US influence.**

## FROM MANIFEST DESTINY TO COLD WAR

The Monroe Doctrine of 1823 laid claim to Latin America and, by implication, Central America and the Caribbean. It was based upon a claim of common interests, coupled with a fear of further European involvement in the area in the wake of the Latin American independence revolutions. But the Monroe Doctrine was also to do with getting an economic foothold in this area so close to the coastline of the United States. Cuba was

**38** The stars and stripes, "Old Glory", flutters over a rural school house in Puerto Rico early in the twentieth century, shortly after it was ceded to the United States.

**39** Teddy Roosevelt (far right), later US President, who led US troops into Cuba at the start of the Spanish-Cuban-American War in 1898.

central to US ambitions at this time. Plans for the annexation or outright purchase of Cuba came to nothing in the nineteenth century. At first, the Spanish would have none of it; then, after the success of the North in the American Civil War, Southern interest in Cuba as a kind of reserve slavocracy evaporated in defeat.

American expansionism at this time, both internally westward as well as outside its own boundaries was couched within the cosy concept of "Manifest Destiny". This was the assertion that the United States had a special responsibility to take its own forms of society, economics and politics to the entirety of the Western Hemisphere. Internally, this can be seen as paternalistic; externally, as later events were to show, it was racialist. By the close of the nineteenth century, the United States, having already challenged the hegemony of Great Britain in Central America, was economically, as well as militarily, equipped to take on an imperial role. Cuba, as we have seen, was the first Caribbean country to feel the unwelcome attentions of the United States – military occupation. Spain's other colony in the Caribbean, Puerto Rico, all that was left of a once mighty Empire in the New World, was the next to fall.

US imperialism was at its most aggressive under the presidency of Theodore (Teddy) Roosevelt and this period has come to be known as the era of "Big Stick" politics, characterized by occupations, interventions, threats of intervention and the wholesale use of coercion. The implicit racialism of the idea of Manifest Destiny was made explicit in Roosevelt's Corollary to the Monroe Doctrine of 1904 which included:

> Chronic wrongdoing or an impotence which results in a general loosening of the ties of civilised society, may in America, as elsewhere, ultimately require intervention by some civilised nation, and in the Western Hemisphere the adherence of the United States to the Monroe Doctrine may force the United States, however reluctantly, in flagrant cases of such wrongdoing or "impotence", to the exercise of an international police power.

The role of the United States as a "police power" has been a consistent thread in its foreign policy towards the region throughout the twentieth century, modified from time to time but consistent nonetheless. As "Teddy" Roosevelt crudely put it himself when referring to Venezuela, the United States had to "show these dagoes that they will have to behave decently".

Acquisition of the Panama Canal Zone, and control of the Canal itself, which was completed in 1914, gave the US a link between its Atlantic and Pacific Coasts and, through control of Puerto Rico and Cuba, the beginnings of control of the Caribbean, later to be an "American Mediterranean". Between 1914 and 1929 American investments in Central America and the Caribbean tripled, with the bulk concentrated in Cuba and Mexico. To safeguard US interests, military occupations as in Cuba, Haiti and the Dominican Republic left no doubt of the seriousness of American intent in the area. Nor did the purchase of the Virgin Islands from the Danish in 1917 for $25 million.

Military interventions, however, were supposed to come to an end with the presidency of Franklin Roosevelt ("FDR") in the 1930s. This was the era of "The Good Neighbour", itself an admission that the US had been a bad neighbour before that time, though neither US threats nor use of force were ever completely abandoned. During the 1933 crisis in Cuba, for example, US warships were positioned off the coast as a form of intimidation. The US government similarly showed its good neighbourliness at this time by supporting some of the most brutal, ruthless dictators the region has ever known: Machado and then Batista in Cuba (Machado was far from affectionately known as "the butcher"); Ubico in Guatemala; Andino in Honduras; Somoza in Nicaragua. However, through its support for men like these, the United States was able to exert its will over the region without needing to use force.

The US presence, already strong in the area, was reinforced during the war years. In Puerto Rico $200 million were spent on the naval base at Roosevelt Roads and the Ramey air force base. US bases in Panama and the Virgin Islands were strengthened. The Destroyers Deal with Britain in 1940 gave the US 99-year leases for bases in Trinidad, Guiana, Antigua, St Lucia, Jamaica and the Bahamas. The countries affected were to be transformed by their contact with "the American way of life". Trinidad, for example, was saturated with US culture, the wealth generated by the base influencing the development of local politics. The Destroyers Deal signalled the end of British control in the area, and the acceptance of American claims to the whole area of the Caribbean. There could be no argument against this claim in the light of America's position of power in the world at the end of the Second World War. Nor was the US loath to use force when necessary, to support its control of the region. This was the case of Guatemala in 1954, the Bay of Pigs in Cuba in 1961, the Dominican Republic in 1965 and Grenada in 1983. The governments, as well as the people, of Grenada and Nicaragua after 1979 have felt the anger of the United States directed along economic lines, as did Michael Manley in Jamaica before 1979. Nor is the US averse to using cruder techniques, such as assassinations, in its attempts to destabilize governments and manipulate the affairs of countries, as many attempts on the life of Fidel Castro throughout the 1960s, and probably beyond, have shown.

It is doubtful if the term "America's Backyard" adds much to our understanding of the region for, whilst American politicians may see it thus, Caribbean people refuse to accept that they are in the subservient position of being in anyone's "backyard". The term hides, too, the involvement of and contribution made by other countries.

# CANADA

Canada's contact and trade with the Caribbean, mainly the old British colonies, are well-established. Traditionally, lumber and fish were traded for sugar and rum, which has led on to a much wider commercial relationship involving machinery, mining, banking and insurance. The traditional commodities are still exchanged, as a visit to any Canadian "Liquor Store" will show.

Canada's relationship with the Caribbean was consolidated in the twentieth century. Trade agreements in 1912, 1920 and 1926 provided advantageous preferential trade to both sides. In 1932 the British Caribbean colonies were included in the Ottawa agreements which gave preferential trading rights to the members of the then British Empire. Canada's insurance and banking spread throughout the Caribbean from the 1890s, as did Canadian shipping aided by government subsidies. Canadian trade and investment in the region have developed substantially from that time, reflecting Canada's own development as well as the growth and development of the Caribbean economies. The Commonwealth Caribbean is by far the largest recipient of Caribbean aid, with investment in the area standing at an estimated US $500 million in the 1980s.

Suriname's bauxite industry was developed with Canadian capital from 1917, rising to some £40 million by 1965. A further £65 million had been put into Jamaica's bauxite industry by the same date. Yet, despite these investments, Canada has not been accused, as has the United States, of being "imperialist" in its dealings with the Caribbean, probably because it has not sought to influence events or to impose its will in the region. However, many of the supposedly Canadian firms, like Alcan, Falconbridge Nickel and Inco, are, in fact, controlled by US capital. It has been suggested that this is a less painful way for further US penetration of the Caribbean.

Canada's relationship with revolutionary Cuba is interesting. Unlike US companies, expropriated Canadian companies and banks received compensation from the revolutionary Cuban government. From the early 1960s Canada's economic links with Cuba have been very useful, given the latter's lack of access to Western, especially US, technology. By 1965 Cuba was already in the top 25 Canadian markets, spending $53 million on Canadian goods. By 1980 this had risen to almost $416 million. The major component of this trade is grain, which Cuba cannot grow itself, as well as a range of machinery and wood products. Cuba's trade to Canada is mostly sugar, along with seafood, cigars and cigarettes. Canada, by the start of the 1980s, had become Cuba's main non-communist trading partner.

# VENEZUELA AND MEXICO

The growth of Venezuelan influence in the Caribbean in the 1970s and 1980s is based entirely upon its oil revenues following the OPEC countries' price rise in 1973. Venezuelan interest in the region caused the late Dr Eric Williams, Prime Minister of Trinidad, to warn of Venezuelan "neo-colonialism". In the 1970s Venezuela, which has a part of its coast actually in the Caribbean, increasingly began to act as a major power in the region, largely motivated to curb the influence of Cuba and show its colours as an ally of the US.

In the period 1978 to 1980 Venezuela placed more than US $450 million worth of aid in the Caribbean, giving loans to Barbados, Guyana and Jamaica. At the same time, Venezuela was dealing a blow to Caribbean hopes of developing its own aluminium smelter, by developing its own capacity based on ores from the region. Trinidad and Tobago had been dealt a similar blow through the unfair competition of Venezuelan oil supplies to the region. This intrusion by Venezuela, a country with great economic power, caused much alarm to the less powerful countries of the Caribbean, especially to the fragile CARICOM.

Mexico has, similarly, shown a greater interest in the Caribbean as a source of raw materials and as a market for its manufactured goods since its own changing fortunes in the 1970s, based on a rise in oil prices. Mexico, unlike Venezuela, has not sought a position of leadership in the area. Rather, through taking a firm position on the need for political solutions to the conflicts in Central America, Mexico has acted as a counter to the strength of the USA. Simply through its size and economic strength, Mexico is bound to exert an influence on the Caribbean as a whole. Up to the 1980s, Mexico has shown a responsible and principled interest in the region.

## THE SOVIET UNION

Before the Cuban Revolution the Soviet Union's role in the Caribbean was virtually non-existent. It was some time, too, before the Soviet Union fully embraced the Cuban Revolution, providing the economic and political lifeline that has sustained it. The relationship between the two countries has not always been harmonious, however; throughout the 1960s the Soviet Union and Cuba were frequently opposed on internal as well as foreign policy. Internally, the Soviet Union was very much opposed to Cuba's stated aim of building communism alongside socialism, especially so since the implication was that Cuba would reach communism before the Soviet Union. Similarly, the USSR disagreed with Cuba's use of moral rather than material incentives to motivate society. On foreign policy there were fundamental disagreements about Cuba's support for liberation and revolutionary groups around the world, especially in Latin America.

**40  British steam engines of the nineteenth century work alongside new advanced Soviet technology in this Cuban sugar mill.**

Relations between the two countries improved dramatically in the early 1970s when the Soviet Union extended favourable economic agreements to Cuba which culminated in 1972 in Cuba's acceptance into COMECON, the Common Market of the Socialist Countries. Without the support of the Soviet Union and the other members of COMECON; without the favourable prices for goods sold to COMECON as well as for commodities, like oil, bought from it; and without credits and gifts of arms and other support, calculated at US$3.5 thousand million a year by the late 1970s/early 1980s, it is doubtful if the standard of living enjoyed by Cubans could have been sustained.

The greater identification of Caribbean nations with the rest of the Third World, which began in the 1970s, has resulted in a much greater contact with all the socialist countries, at economic levels and at the world's political meeting places like the Non-Aligned Movement. The Soviet Union has extended moderate support to Caribbean countries. To Michael Manley in Jamaica the USSR extended credits and other economic assistance, at the same time counselling moderation by advising Manley to stay in the capitalist camp. Credits and expertise were similarly offered to the New Jewel Movement in Grenada for the airport and other projects. Guyana has trade agreements with the Soviet Union for sugar and bauxite, in return for timber and heavy machinery.

Although these Soviet links with the Caribbean are not considerable, they nonetheless raise the suspicions of the United States government which is concerned at the "spread of communism" within the region and especially in Central America. Cuba and the Soviet Union are jointly held

responsible for this, although convincing evidence to support the assertion has not been provided by the US government. There are grounds for thinking that rather than actively encouraging revolution, as Cuba undoubtedly did in the 1960s, Cuba and the Soviet Union have played a restraining role over radical governments in the Caribbean. Nonetheless, US foreign policy is based upon the assumption of an expansionist role for the Soviet Union and Cuba.

## THE CARIBBEAN BASIN INITIATIVE

The Caribbean Basin Initiative (CBI) was the initiative of Edward Seaga, the Prime Minister of Jamaica in 1980, and has been described as a "mini Marshall Plan for the Caribbean". The idea of the initiative is to channel US funds to Central America and the Caribbean. Development is not the aim of the CBI for, as President Reagan made clear when announcing the project in February 1982, it was part of the US government's strategy to prevent further revolutionary gains in the area:

> If we do not act promptly and decisively in defence of freedom, new Cubas will arise from the ruins of today's conflict.

When the plan was unveiled, Jamaica, a close ally of the United States, had been singled out for special attention, getting $110 million out of $350 million. The other Caribbean countries saw this disparity as being at the expense of and to the detriment of themselves. CARICOM members, other than Jamaica, put their concerns to President Reagan during his visit to Jamaica and Barbados at Easter 1982. The exclusion of Grenada from the project was seen as especially divisive to CARICOM, whilst the bad-blood between Havana and Washington was seen as nothing to do with the rest of the Caribbean.

Nor did President Reagan have an easy path with the CBI in his own government, which forced upon him fundamental amendments. The legislation for the bill was finally signed by President Reagan in August 1983. Rather than being a highly publicized affair, the coming into being of the CBI turned out to be a damp squib. The slow passage of the bill through the US legislature had embarrassed Caribbean leaders as well as the President himself. The pointed and divisive exclusion of Grenada, Guyana, Nicaragua and Cuba from the project remained; nor is Bahamas likely to benefit, since to do so would require changes to the secrecy of its banking laws. It is unlikely that the CBI will make any fundamental contribution to a solution of the Caribbean region's problems, although some countries close to the US, such as Jamaica and Barbados, may have received some marginal relief.

Even these countries' position could change. In November 1983 Edward Seaga announced a devaluation of the Jamaican dollar and a general election, hoping to benefit from the "Grenada factor". Had the People's National Party, led by Michael Manley, stood in this election and had they won, it is unlikely that the CBI would have benefited Jamaica. In November 1983 Barbados was in dispute with the US over the American government's decision to unilaterally break an agreement on taxation.

## YOUNG HISTORIAN

**A**

1 Find out more about the Monroe Doctrine, and the ideas behind Manifest Destiny.
2 Why was the United States so interested in Cuba in the nineteenth century?
3 What do you understand by the term "Imperialism"? Has the United States played an imperialist role in the Caribbean?
4 Why have Caribbean countries in recent times shown an interest in trade with many countries?
5 Can the Caribbean Basin Initiative (CBI) be an answer to the economic problems of the Caribbean? If not, what are the answers to these problems?

**B**

1 Imagine you can interview "Teddy" Roosevelt in Cuba in 1898. What questions would you ask him?
2 You are a Spaniard living in Cuba at the end of the nineteenth century. How do you view the arrival of US troops?

**C**

1 Compose headlines for (a) the US purchase of the Virgin Islands, (b) the announcement of "The Good Neighbour Policy", (c) the US defeat at the Bay of Pigs, (d) Cuba's success at the Bay of Pigs.

**D**

On a map of the Caribbean show US interventions, US trade or aid, US possessions.

# REVOLUTIONARY ALTERNATIVES

On 26 July 1953 Fidel Castro led an attack on the Moncada Barracks at Santiago de Cuba. The attack was a failure, Fidel Castro was imprisoned, many of his followers were killed. Yet just five years later Fidel Castro, released from prison, had returned to Cuba from exile and "had the dictator beheaded at [my] feet" as he had said he would. The Cuban Revolution began on 1 January 1959; its effects are still being felt throughout Latin America and the Caribbean.

**41 Fidel Castro, on the far right, at his arrest in July 1953 following the failed attack on the Moncada Barracks in Santiago de Cuba.**

## THE CUBAN REVOLUTION

The Cuban Revolution celebrated its first quarter century on 1 January 1984. In those 25 years Cuban society has been transformed from "the whorehouse of the Caribbean", with Havana shared equally between corrupt politicians and the Mafia, to a socialist form of organization within which there are still hardships but in which the people of Cuba can live fulfilling lives with dignity.

Before 1959 Havana gobbled up resources at the expense of the countryside. All that has now changed in Cuba. Positive discrimination in

favour of the countryside has resulted in new developments such as new schools and clinics, new hospitals and factories, new farms, even new rural communities. No area of the countryside, however remote, is without adequate medical and educational provision. The parasites and epidemics which were the killers in the past have been replaced by diseases more associated with developed countries. The ignorance of the past has been similarly eradicated; now Cuba even exports its expertise to those countries less well off than itself. Yet many of the problems from the past continue to assert themselves.

Cuban Sugar; once, the two words were synonomous, and sugar still occupies the most important place in the Cuban economy. Sugar will remain the most important sector in the economy until the year 2000; new mills are to be built, others renovated so as to produce even more each year. Yet in the first years of the revolution canefields were ploughed up to make room for any other crop than sugar, in order to get away from the position of dependence on the United States that the production of sugar implied. Most Cuban sugar went to the US market under the Quota System, whereby sugar-producing countries in the area were allotted a proportion of US imports of sugar, a quota, according to the closeness of the relationship existing between the two countries at that time. Through the Quota System the US could exert great political, as well as economic pressure, on the sugar-producing countries who were part of the system. However, Cuba was unable to get away from sugar as easily as planned. Changing sugar cane areas into land for other crops resulted in a decline in agricultural production.

The attempt to get away from sugar, a lesson in itself for the rest of the Caribbean sugar-producers, was linked to an ambitious and unrealistic attempt to industrialize. This, too, was a tragic waste of resources. By 1964 Cuba had abandoned its attempts at rapid industrialization and was once again a major producer of sugar. This time, however, it was to produce even more sugar than before. Why? Fidel Castro explained in 1970:

> . . . we proposed a long-term sugar export agreement to the Soviet Union, an agreement that would help meet the growing needs presented by our economy – and especially by our development.
> Sugar was practically the only product whose

export we could increase rapidly. First because there was a certain amount of underutilized industrial capacity. Second, because there were many sugar mills which could increase their production with relatively small investments in new equipment . . . . Moreover, we could lengthen the harvest period.

So, by 1970 Cuba set itself to produce ten million tons of sugar (more than had ever been produced in Cuba's history before), by gradually increasing each year's harvest. Industrialization was to proceed at a more modest pace.

The "Battle for the Ten Million Tons" was to end in failure, too, despite the massive and heroic efforts put into the project by the Cuban people. Soldiers were drafted into the cane fields, workers were seconded to cut cane, teachers and students joined them at weekends. Yet the target was not reached. Not only this, but the whole Cuban economy had been dislocated in the attempt. Fidel Castro took much of the blame himself:

> I am in no way trying to pin the blame on anyone not in the revolutionary leadership and myself.
> I believe that we, the leaders of this Revolution, have cost the party too much in our process of learning . . .
> One of our most difficult problems . . . is our heritage of ignorance . . . and I, of course, am not the exception.

Partly because of Cuba's shortfall in production, the price rose in the early 1970s. By 1974/75 the price had risen to the exalted level of 66 cents per pound, only to crash thereafter and remain at a low level into the 1980s. Cuba, along with other Third World sugar-producers, was being adversely affected by the huge amounts of subsidized beet sugar produced by the EEC. Fidel Castro has spoken out at international fora on the acute problems facing primary-producing countries like Cuba, especially in the context of expenditures on arms by the developed world. The arms trade constitutes a considerable burden on the weak economies of the underdeveloped countries. It is the most sterile, unproductive and unequal exchange for those countries. The arms trade deprives the importing country of resources that could be used for productive activities.

> The cost of a modern bomber prototype equals the salaries of 250,000 teachers for one year, or the construction and equipment cost of 75 hospitals with 100 beds each. The price of a Trident nuclear submarine equals the annual cost of sending 16

**42   Until the late 1970s the technology employed in Cuban sugar mills dated from the late nineteenth/ early twentieth century. This has now been replaced.**

million children to school in underdeveloped countries, or the cost of building 400,000 homes for 2 million people. The money spent on a modern tank could pay for the construction of 1,000 classrooms for 30,000 children in Third World countries.

Yet Cuba is unique in the Caribbean, in that its agreements with the Soviet Union and other COMECON countries provide guaranteed prices for goods bought as well as products sold. It is for that reason, perhaps, that Cuban sugar will remain the most important sector in the economy to the year 2000.

Alone in the Caribbean Cuba has been able to successfully deal with many of the social problems that have plagued the area. In education, Cuba has been conspicuously successful, transforming a country with high rates of illiteracy and a dismal record of education provision into one which is now able to export its achievements in education. Illiteracy was attacked in the Literacy Campaign of 1961, which put students and teachers in the homes of illiterate people, beginning the process of further and continuing education that continues in the 1980s. The "Battle for the Sixth Grade", designed to bring every adult up to 6th Grade, Elementary level, was successfully concluded in 1980. Now the country is embarked upon the "Battle for the 9th Grade", Secondary level.

The main importance given to education in the first years of the revolution has, if anything, gained momentum over the 25 years. At Elementary level, Cuba has all its students at school, many in new, purpose-built schools and others using schools remaining from earlier times or sometimes, even, expropriated houses. All schools combine study with work. At Elementary schools, this consists of a token one hour a day of gentle work. At Secondary level, half the day is spent in the classroom, the other half on some productive activity. Most Secondary students go to schools in the country, co-educational boarding schools with their own agricultural land that is worked by the staff and students. This is a way for a poor country like Cuba to afford a high quality of education for all. It is also a way of developing a respect for work. Future generations, it is hoped, will be flexible and adaptable, fitting into whatever the task of the Revolution happens to be. Two schools like this were built in Jamaica, as a gift from the Cuban people, during the period in the 1970s when Michael Manley was Prime Minister.

Cuba's educational achievements are matched by those in health. Cuba now exports doctors and nurses to other Third World countries. Cuban medical teams are working in the Caribbean in Guyana and Nicaragua and were working in Jamaica until 1979 and in Grenada until 1983. Cuba's success in health has been the result of

61

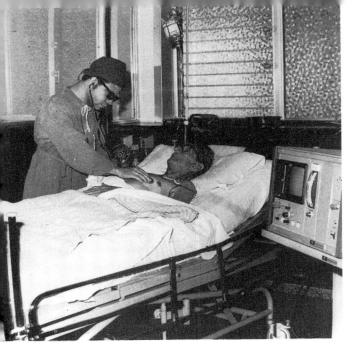

**43** Health and education have been priorities in the Cuban Revolution from its inception in 1959. Cuban doctors and nurses have worked in a number of Caribbean countries.

increasing the volume of care through more doctors and nurses and more hospitals and polyclinics; but, importantly as well, it has been the result of improvements in education, housing and diet. Cuba shares its expertise in health and education by offering scholarships to the Third World. Many Caribbean students are therefore studying in Cuba.

Fidel Castro has played a crucial role in the overall transformation of Cuba. Until the 1970s he was *the* most important political figure, taking control personally of a wide range of economic as well as political matters. This personal style of leadership was, perhaps, inevitable in the first years of revolution. By the 1970s, however, there had developed in Cuba a large number of experienced, credible figures who could also take on some of the decision-making. The country moved towards developing revolutionary institutions of government.

Cuba, in the first half of the 1970s, was a country preoccupied with discussing the forms of new political institutions. Workers discussed the role of trade unions. Did they even have a role in a socialist society? Each neighbourhood organization – the CDRs (Committees for the Defence of the Revolution) – met to discuss its own role and then the new draft Constitution and the

Family Code which set out the responsibilities of partners in marriage and the rights of children. The membership of the Cuban Communist Party was increased during this time and, in the process, the Party was democratized through the inclusion of a wider representation of Cuban society.

The system of government that emerged in the 1970s was *People's Power,* which was designed to decentralize decision-making, putting economic and political power into the hands of the people living in the 14 new administrative divisions of the country. Municipal Assemblies, at which delegates elected by their constituents sit, are responsible for the administration of a wide range of goods and services in each municipality. Delegates to the Provincial and National Assemblies are elected by delegates in the assemblies below them, in the pyramid of assemblies. At the point of the pyramid sits the Council of State, over which Fidel Castro presides. In effect, Fidel Castro became the President of Cuba in 1976.

## A GRENADAN REVOLUTION

The New Jewel Movement (NJM) led by Maurice Bishop referred to the "revolution" occurring in Grenada, but if it was a revolution, it was a very different one from the Cuban model. To

**44** Maurice Bishop of Grenada and Fidel Castro in Santiago de Cuba to celebrate the 30th Anniversary of Fidel Castro's attack on the Moncada Barracks.

understand what happened in Grenada, we must first look at what preceded the seizure of power by the NJM in 1979.

Eric Gairy came to prominence in Grenada in the 1950s as a trade union organizer, then as a political leader. In 1950 Gairy registered his new trade union, the Grenada Manual and Mental Workers Union (GMMWU), with himself as President-General, and immediately began to agitate for higher wages in the agricultural industries – sugar, cocoa and nutmeg. When these demands were rebuffed, Gairy organized strikes and, in 1951, the first national strike in Grenada's history. The strike was successful, largely because of its violent nature, with arson and looting commonplace. Gairy encouraged the violence, using the code word "sky-red" whenever he wanted an estate burned. Finally imprisoned by Grenada's Governor, Gairy assumed the role of both hero and martyr. The violence continued until he was released to put an end to it. It was an opportunity for Gairy to enhance his own prestige and personal power:

> Yes folks, this is your leader, "Uncle Gairy" speaking to you. My dear, fellow Grenadians, you know that I am deeply concerned over the present state of affairs in our dear little island. You too – everyone of you – are concerned one way or another. As head of Grenada's two largest organizations – the Grenada People's Party and the Grenada Mental and Manual Workers' Union, I feel obliged morally and spiritually to alleviate, to stop, and when I say stop, I mean stop the burning of buildings and fields; interfering with people who are breaking your strikes. Stop taking things away from the estates that are not belonging to you, particularly cocoa and nutmeg.

Gairy then moved from trade union agitation to political organization. He organized the Grenada People's Party (GPP), in readiness for the 1951 elections. Helped by the full vote that had been introduced the previous year, his party was swept to victory. In less than a year Gairy had emerged from nowhere to become Grenada's new leader. His role was described by a Grenadan historian:

> Gairy's appearance on the scene was like a Messiah, one who came at a particular time to save his people from oppression and open a new era of hope.

Gairy certainly represented a new spirit in Grenada in which working people felt themselves caught up, with Gairy taking on their demands. More than that, black people could identify with their own champion.

In the 1950s Gairy lost interest in the GMMWU, his important power base, concerning himself instead with "astral influences", supernatural powers and Obeah – a form of witchcraft. As a result, he lost the 1957 election to his former partner, Hubert Blaize, who had organized the Grenada National Party (GNP). Unable to stand in the 1961 election because of his rowdy behaviour in those of 1957, Gairy backed Joshua Thorne as head of his new Grenada United Labour Party (GULP), but Thorne, on election, resigned, to allow Gairy to take over as Chief Minister of State. Within a year, Gairy's corruption and squandering of public funds resulted in a new election which was won by the GNP. Gairy had to wait until 1967 before winning power again.

The years from 1937 to 1979, with Gairy in power, saw Grenada converted into a dictatorship, the cult of personality – Gairy's, and wholesale corruption. Grenada became Gairy's personal estate, with his approval required for every decision, however minute. He maintained himself in power by force and repression through the use of thugs, the Mongoose Gang and the Green Beasts. He concerned himself increasingly with fringe religions based on witchcraft, and with flying saucers.

The economy crumbled. Prices rose while wages hardly moved. Medical care was insufficient and expensive. Education became a privilege. Not surprisingly, there developed challenges to Gairy, the first being a Black Power rally in sympathy with a revolt taking place in Trinidad. Gairy responded to strikes and other challenges to his rule by massively increasing the State's repressive apparatus.

The New Jewel Movement, formed in 1973, rapidly became a credible challenge to Gairyism. When its leaders were viciously attacked at a meeting by Gairy's thugs, popular revulsion at his methods signalled a turning point in his career. It was now a question of time before Gairy was ousted. In the meantime, Gairy used Grenada's independence from Britain in 1974 to his own advantage. Labelling his opposition "communist", he began to champion the causes of repressive regimes like Pinochet's in Chile. At the same time,

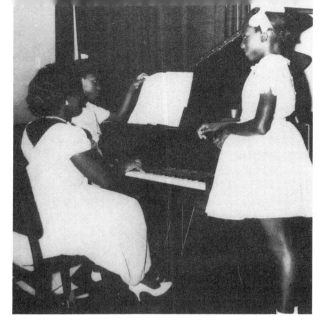

**45** Mrs Gairy, wife of Prime Minister Gairy of Grenada, sits at the piano allegedly paid for by Gairy from diverted state funds.

**46** Protests against Eric Gairy's violations of human rights in Grenada led to the movement that ousted him in 1979.

the economy continued to stagnate, with 50% of the workforce unemployed. Gairy clung on to power through thuggery and rigging elections.

The NJM organized for the overthrow of Gairy through its People's Revolutionary Army (PRA), armed by supporters in Gairy's army and police force. When they learned, in March 1979, that Gairy intended to liquidate the leadership of the NJM, they decided to act. On the morning of 13 March 1979 the PRA took the army barracks at True Blue, razing it to the ground. In under twelve

hours the NJM had taken power. Gairy, in New York, had been ousted.

The Grenadan people rose in support of the NJM. Maurice Bishop, who had been brutally treated by Gairy's thugs, became the new Prime Minister. He announced the NJM's intentions:

> People of Grenada, this revolution is for work, for food, for decent housing and health services, and for a bright future for our children and our grandchildren. The benefits of the revolution will be given to everyone regardless of political opinion or which political party they support. Let us all unite as one.

Feelings in the rest of the Caribbean towards the new government in Grenada were mixed. There had been universal repugnance to Gairyism, but the NJM was an unknown quantity. Official recognition came early from the larger islands, Jamaica, Barbados, Trinidad and Guyana. Cuba embraced the revolution enthusiastically. By contrast, the smaller Eastern Caribbean states were fearful of a "revolution" on their doorstep. The NJM and the Provisional Revolutionary Government soon became the target for US government accusations of Cuban and Soviet involvement in the affairs of the country. The US Ambassador to the Eastern Caribbean warned Bishop of too close a liaison with Cuba and the USSR. Bishop's response was clear:

> From day one of the revolution we have always striven to have and develop the closest and friendliest relations with the United States, as well as Canada, Britain, and all our Caribbean neighbours. But no one must misunderstand our friendliness as an excuse for rudeness and meddling in our affairs, and no one, no matter how mighty and powerful they are, will be permitted to dictate to the government and people of Grenada who we can have friendly terms with and what kind of relations we must have with other countries.
>
> We are not in anyone's backyard.

The next day Grenada established diplomatic relations with Cuba and the first Cuban aid began to arrive. From that time on Grenada was viewed with suspicion and hostility by the United States. Attempts at destabilizing Grenada were made through the blocking of international funds and a diplomatic offensive against the country. An overt attack on the PRG came in 1980 when a bomb exploded at a public rally, under the government speakers' platform. None of the cabinet ministers

**47 How Grenadans saw the threat of a US invasion in 1981.**

on the platform was harmed, but two women were killed and nearly a hundred injured.

A major bone of contention between Grenada and the US was the use to which the international airport on Grenada would be put. The PRG insisted it was for tourism and for shipping goods in and out of the country. US fears were that it could be used by Cuba or the USSR. One effect of the American attitude was to make the airport the most publicized in the Caribbean.

Grenada needed change after the corruption and mismanagement of Gairy, but while the PRG could put a stop to the legacy of waste and corruption, there was little to be done in the short term, to change the well-established structural problems of the economy. Bernard Coard, Grenada's Minister of Finance, explained:

> We depend almost entirely on [the] advanced countries to buy all our cocoa, nutmegs and bananas. We also depend on them to supply us with most of the things we cannot produce and must buy from abroad. In fact, our economy is so tied to the economies of these countries that there is a long-standing joke which says that anytime the economy in one of these countries coughs, *we* must catch the cold. The economies of these countries started coughing since the end of 1978 and they are still coughing in 1981. And we have caught a serious cold which we still have to get over.

To break out of its historical role as supplier of cheap agricultural products, Grenada developed a system of self-sufficiency, by producing its own foodstuffs, buying less from abroad and diversifying and increasing domestic production. The PRG did not nationalize the private sector which worked alongside the State sector. In tourism, for example, the State ran hotels, recovered from Gairy, alongside private hotels. The State took a hand in economic planning for the first time in Grenada, as a way of developing the country and bringing a better standard of living for Grenadians. What the PRG did hardly constituted a revolution, neither was it socialist in the sense that the Cuban revolution is socialist.

Discussion about the nature of the Grenadan revolution was made academic in October 1983 with the coup led by Bernard Coard that resulted in the death of Maurice Bishop and paved the way for the invasion of Grenada by United States military forces. The invasion was enthusiastically supported by the leaders of Jamaica, Barbados, Dominica and the other tiny islands of the Eastern Caribbean. Trinidad and Guyana and the remainder of CARICOM members were as violently opposed to the invasion, preferring to see Caribbean countries arrive at their own destinies. Cuba was particularly caught up in the invasion. The Cuban government, and especially Fidel Castro, were very close to the PRG led by Maurice Bishop; Bishop himself was much revered by the Cuban people; Cubans were working in Grenada on a number of projects and fought back when fired upon by the invading forces.

**48 The beautiful natural harbour of St Georges, Grenada, before the US invasion of 1983.**

The invasion of Grenada was presented to American people as a victory for President Reagan's foreign policy against Cuba and the Soviet Union and against the revolutionary movement. It came immediately after the tragic deaths of 240 US Marines, part of a peace-keeping force, in Beirut. In the wake of this particular tragedy, and of past foreign policy setbacks for the US government, the majority of American public opinion rallied in support of the President. In a speech in Havana, on 14 November 1983, commemorating the 24 Cubans who died in Grenada, Fidel Castro asked:

> Where is the glory, the grandeur and the victory in invading and defeating one of the tiniest countries in the world, of no economic or strategic significance?... In its efforts to destroy a symbol, the United States killed a corpse and brought the symbol back to life at the same time.

In November 1983 President Reagan spoke of his determination to "bring the boys home for Christmas". The civilian airport at Point Salines was being converted into a military airstrip. Bernard Coard who had led the coup against Bishop was imprisoned. Soviet and Cuban technicians had been forced to return home. It was announced that American casualties had been even higher than those suffered by the Cubans. Eric Gairy announced his intention to return to Grenadan politics. The figures for Grenadan deaths in the invasion were still unknown.

---

## SOCIALISM IN JAMAICA?

---

The People's National Party (PNP) led by Michael Manley came to power in Jamaica in 1972. It soon initiated a number of reforms like free secondary education, a literacy campaign and a limited land reform. In 1974 Manley published his *Politics of Change* which was his blueprint for the social transformation of Jamaica. In it he advocated a system of participatory democracy and put forward his critique of capitalism and imperialism. Manley saw the need to develop the confidence of the Jamaican people for change. Any possibilities for change were severely curtailed by economic factors – domestic inflation and the

world economic crisis. Nor was Manley successful in deriving greater revenues from bauxite producers; they simply cut their consumption from Jamaica. Manley's relationship with Cuba and his support for the MPLA in Angola at the same time gained him the antagonism of the US government, which blocked his application for aid and interfered with would-be sources of credit. Equally serious was the decrease in tourists to Jamaica from the US, warned off by their government. Despite this American interference and the violent campaign of Manley's opposition, the Jamaican Labour Party (JLP), Manley received a landslide victory in the 1976 elections.

**49 Fidel Castro's visit to Jamaica in 1978 was one expression of the contacts that existed between Cuba and Jamaica in the 1970s in the political, economic and social fields.**

Economic problems forced Manley into the arms of the International Monetary Fund (IMF), which imposed on Jamaica a drastic cutback in public spending, a wage freeze and the devaluation of the Jamaican dollar. Manley lost a great deal of his support. IMF = IT MANLEY FAULT became a common piece of graffiti. Manley moved from the left, to the right, and back to the left again. All to no avail; the JLP won the 1980 election with the biggest majority in Jamaican history. The JLP election success was almost certainly the result of assistance provided by the US government, which made no secret of its support for Edward Seaga, Jamaica's new Prime Minister, though four years after the election the hoped-for revitalization of the Jamaican economy had not appeared. In November 1983 Prime Minister Seaga called a general election, after devaluing the Jamaican dollar. The PNP decided not to contest it.

## THE SANDINISTA REVOLUTION IN NICARAGUA

US support for Edward Seaga in Jamaica was the more readily given because of the overthrow of Somoza in Nicaragua in the year before the 1980 election. Somoza had been supported by the US, but finally he could only depend upon his own family and cronies grouped around him. His vicious rule gained him the enmity and loathing of every neighbouring government, as well as that of his own countrymen.

The Sandinistas were, on many occasions since their foundation in 1960, on the brink of annihilation, but each time came through to enlarge their support. Their struggle against Somoza was instrumental in generating a consciousness that favoured radical change. The speed of their final success over Somoza and the National Guard surprised even the Sandinistas themselves. As in Grenada, the Nicaraguan revolution has a place for the private sector and considerable personal freedoms. Its ideology of revolution has a strong religious component. Like Grenada, it too has incurred the wrath of Washington, which has effectively cut off sources of international aid and credits, at the same time

as supporting the Contras – the counter revolutionaries who are launching attacks across Nicaragua's borders. Manoeuvres by the US fleet off the coast of Nicaragua have done nothing to calm fears that it intends to blockade the coast or even invade the country. The economic, social and political problems facing the Sandinistas in 1979 were massive; combined with the antagonism of the United States they seem insurmountable.

## COUP IN SURINAME

Unlike in Grenada and Nicaragua the winds of change that blew in Suriname came from the Right rather than from the Left. The coup which occurred in Suriname in February 1980, but which had been planned during the two years previously, was organized by elements within the military. The disparate groups which took part in the coup, each with different political positions and ambitions, have contributed to the instability that has characterized Suriname's society since then.

Throughout the 1970s tension grew in Suriname. Poverty had increased whilst the wealthier sections of society got wealthier. Nor did the 1974 crisis in the world aluminium industry, Suriname's most important export industry, help matters. Unemployment rose along with inflation. Emigration to Holland took on astronomical proportions. In 1975 Suriname's independence from Holland was accompanied by a 6 million Guilders package of aid to contribute to the country's development. New hydro-electric projects were to be built, alumina and aluminium plants established, even a new city was to be built. Independence and the influx of capital for development raised Suriname's expectations. They were not to be met. Emigration rose again in 1978, depriving the country of much-needed skilled workers. The government, led by Prime Minister Henk Arron, despite pressure to stop the flow of expertise, took no action.

The economic and social crisis of Suriname was reinforced by a succession of corruption scandals involving the government. Ministers were arrested and tried. Suspicion of the Arron government grew. From 1978 resistance to the government developed over a number of issues:

Indians demonstrated violently over the loss of their lands; youth organizations agitated for a lowering of the age of entitlement to vote; trade unions fought for wage increases to match inflation. Even the churches mobilized against the government's policies which discriminated in favour of the rich. Socialist influences were felt in the church and elsewhere. Most damaging for Arron's government's chances of survival was the opposition that was growing in trade and industrial quarters, hard-hit by the government's indifference and lack of support. Much-needed incentives to local trade and industry had not been forthcoming, whilst foreign firms were growing fat on funds available for Suriname's development. Left, right and centre, opposition to the government grew.

Discontent erupted in the military with the formation of a union – Bomika – which made repeated demands for improvements in their conditions. The government and military leadership ignored the demands, and this led to a physical confrontation between the two sides. The government's intransigence did much to provoke the coup of 1980. Bomika's fight for union rights had the effect of invigorating other sections of society – other trade unions, women's groups, youth organizations – to push for their demands. The great mass of society was now, for different reasons, opposed to the government.

The physical overthrow of Arron's government had been openly discussed since 1976. Such a course now seemed the only option. The military made their move ousting Arron, setting up the National Military Council (NMC) and quickly acting to control opposition through press censorship, curfews and a ban on political meetings. Despite these moves, the new regime has been characterized by instability since the successful outcome of the coup. Internal dissent has led to tensions within the NMC as well as there being pressure from outside the country. Internal tensions erupted in December 1983, resulting in the deaths of 13 leading political activists and this hardened the already hard-line of Holland which cut off aid to Suriname. The US, too, has been identified by the NMC as adding to its pressures and it is likely that the US government was behind Brazil's 1983 offer to provide funds and expertise in return for Suriname cutting its links with countries like Grenada, Nicaragua and Cuba. Following the invasion of Grenada, the NMC expelled Cubans in Suriname.

## YOUNG HISTORIAN

**A**

1 Why did Fidel Castro attack the Moncada Barracks in 1953? Why did the attack fail?
2 Write a short biography of Che Guevara.
3 What are the reasons for Cuba's involvement in Africa?
4 How, and why, are study and work combined in Cuban education?
5 Find out more about Maurice Bishop.
6 Why did Michael Manley lose power in Jamaica?

**B**

1 Fidel Castro gives very few interviews but you have been selected to interview him for radio and television. What twelve questions would you ask him, bearing in mind that he is unwilling to answer questions about his personal life?
2 Imagine you are in the mountains with Fidel Castro's Rebel Army in the 1950s. Write about a typical day.

**C**

1 Compose headlines for (a) the Moncada Attack, (b) Batista's flight from Cuba, (c) the Cuban Missile Crisis, (d) the death of Maurice Bishop.

**D**

Design a sculpture to commemorate *either* Che Guevara *or* Maurice Bishop.

# THE WAY FORWARD

The invasion of Grenada reinforced trends that were already under way in the Caribbean from the start of the twentieth century. This intervention by the United States in the Eastern Caribbean, one of a long line of such invasions, was the reaffirmation, if one were needed, of its hegemony in the affairs of Caribbean people. It was also an indication of the lengths to which the United States was prepared to go in pursuit of its aims.

The invasion brought to the surface further divisions, which were already simmering within CARICOM, with potentially destructive consequences. The invasion raised the spectre for Cuba and Nicaragua of the possibilities of invasion of their own territories.

American control was further reinforced by the stated intention of the British government to withdraw its troops from Belize. The United States, already militarily committed in Belize, is willing to take Britain's place.

## CRISIS IN THE CARIBBEAN?

The Caribbean has been described as a region in "crisis" in the 1980s. Whether one accepts this extreme label or not, the fact remains that the region's economies, because of their close integration with more powerful, developed countries, have suffered disproportionately from

**50  Cuban cartoons about the subservient roles of Edward Seaga, Prime Minister of Jamaica, and of Sir Paul Scoon, the Governor General of Grenada, show graphically the Cuban attitude to US influence in the region following the invasion of Grenada.**

the world's economic crisis. Caribbean countries are caught within the scissor-blades of falling prices for their primary goods, like sugar and tobacco, and rising prices for the manufactured goods they wish to buy. Tourism, linked to the prosperity of the more affluent countries of the world, has declined as that prosperity has faded.

Standards of living in the Caribbean, far from rising, have fallen, bringing into question the political and economic systems followed by the region's governments. With the increasing identification of the Caribbean with the Third World's general demands for an end to poverty and the pursuit of policies that will signal a start to economic and social development, traditional policies are likely to become increasingly questioned. Only through unity and co-operation in the Caribbean can change come about. Structures to bring about economic and political co-operation, of which CARICOM is but one, do exist; yet the division and rivalries of earlier times are still very much in evidence in the 1980s. The risk of continuing with such attitudes is that nationalism and isolation will increase, with Caribbean countries played off against each other, adding a further twist to the instability, inequality and the racial and other divisions that have long been the realities of Caribbean history.

# Some Facts About the Caribbean

| State | Population (1981) | %Urban | Language | Per Capita Income 1981 (US $) | Size (square miles) | Capital | Economy |
|---|---|---|---|---|---|---|---|
| Cuba | 9.9 million | 74% | Spanish | 1,410 | 44,218 | Havana | Sugar, nickel, tobacco, tourism |
| Haiti | 5.5 million | 20% | French | 260 | 10,714 | Port-au-Prince | Bauxite, tourism, coffee |
| Dominican Republic | 5.5 million | 64% | Spanish | 990 | 18,816 | Santo-Domingo | Bauxite, tourism, coffee, tobacco |
| Puerto Rico | 3.2 million | 58% | Spanish | 2,970 | 3,435 | San-Juan | Bananas, sugar, citrus, coffee, oil refining industry, tourism |
| Martinique | 340,000 | 67% | French | 4,680 | 425 | Fort-de-France | Bananas, tourism, citrus, sugar |
| Guadeloupe | 325,000 | 67% | French | 3,260 | 687 | Basse-Terre | Bananas, tourism, citrus, sugar |
| Guyane | 63,000 | | French | 2,580 | | Cayenne | Citrus, sugar, timber, aluminium, bauxite |
| Dutch Antilles (Aruba, Curacao, Bonaire) | 250,000 | | Dutch | 4,680 | | | Coffee, tobacco, tourism |
| Suriname | 350,000 | | Dutch | 2,360 | | Paramaribo | Bauxite, rice, bananas, citrus, sugar |
| Bahamas | 213,000 | | English | 2,780 | 4,403 | Nassau | Tourism |
| Barbados | 250,000 | 4% | English | 2,400 | 166 | Bridgetown | Tourism, sugar, rum, tobacco, manufacturing |
| Guyana (formerly British Guiana) | 795,000 | 40% | English | 570 | | Georgetown | Bauxite, sugar, rice, timber, alumina |

| State | Population (1981) | %Urban | Language | Per Capita Income 1981 (US $) | Size (square miles) | Capital | Economy |
|---|---|---|---|---|---|---|---|
| Jamaica | 2.2 million | 37% | English | 1,240 | 4,411 | Kingston | Bauxite, tourism, sugar, bananas, citrus, tobacco, manufacturing |
| Trinidad & Tobago | 1.1 million | 12% | English | 3,390 | 1,980 | Port-of-Spain | Oil, asphalt, sugar, citrus, coffee, cocoa, natural gas, manufacturing |
| Antigua & Barbuda | 76,000 | | English | 1,070 | 108 & 62½ | St John's | Sugar, cotton, tourism |
| Belize (formerly British Honduras) | 148,000 | | English | 1,030 | | Belize | Tobacco, citrus, timber |
| Dominica | 80,000 | | English | 410 | 305 | Roseau | Bananas, citrus, tourism |
| Grenada | 111,000 | | English | 630 | 133 | St George's | Bananas, nutmegs, tourism, cocoa |
| Montserrat | 12,000 | | English | | 39½ | Plymouth | Cotton, tourism |
| St Kitts/Nevis | 49,000 | | English | 780 | 68 & 36 | Basseterre & Charlestown | Sugar, cotton, tourism |
| St Lucia | 120,000 | | English | 780 | 238 | Castries | Bananas, tourism |
| St Vincent | 116,000 | | English | 490 | 150 | Kingstown | Bananas, tourism, arrowroot |
| Anguilla | 6,600 | | English | | 35 | | Cotton, tourism |
| British Virgin Islands | 12,200 | | English | | 60 | Roadtown | Tourism |
| Cayman Islands | 16,800 | | English | | 100 | Georgetown | Tourism, banking |
| Turks & Caicos | 7,500 | | English | | 169 | Grand Turk | Tourism |
| US Virgin Islands | 58,000 | | English | 5,580 | 133 | Charlotte Amalia | Tourism |

# INDEX

The numbers in **bold type** refer to figure numbers of the illustrations